Study Guide
to
Jewish Ethics

A Reader's Companion to
Matters of Life and Death,
To Do the Right and the Good,
Love Your Neighbor and Yourself

Paul Steinberg

2003 • 5764
The Jewish Publication Society
Philadelphia

The Jewish Publication Society
2100 Arch Street, 2nd floor
Philadelphia, PA 19103

Edited by Candace Levy
Designed and typeset by Janice Cane

Manufactured in the United States of America

03 04 05 06 07 08 09 10   10 9 8 7 6 5 4 3 2 1

Contents

Introduction

Hashkiveinu. Help us, God, to lie down in peace and awaken us again to life, our Ruler. Spread over Your shelter of peace, guide us with Your good counsel. Save us because of Your mercy. Shield us from enemies and pestilence, from starvation, sword, and sorrow. Remove the evil forces that surround us, shelter us in the shadow of Your wings.

This portion of a Jewish prayer, which is recited in the evening, expresses thoughts and feelings that resonate with most people. It speaks of the dream that most of us have: that we will live in peace with supreme guidance, "happily ever after." We all know, however, that this remains only a dream, as most do not experience a life of complete peace, neither physically nor psychologically. As we look around at our communities and greater society, we cannot help but notice the pain. We see the pain caused by war and violence, by poverty, and by a lack of communal compassion and understanding evidenced by prejudice of race, religion, gender, and sexual orientation.

Even within our own homes, we find some matters of life painful. We sense the sorrow and frustration of couples who find themselves unable to experience the joy of having a child together, we are aware of the tragedy of abuse that occurs within some families, and we are often overwhelmed when a loved one endures a long, drawn-out illness that results in an unpleasant death.

These sorts of problems flood our minds with questions. What can we do? What should we do? What are we expected to do? These are moral questions that focus on what is right and/or good and what it is that we are responsible for.

Moral issues such as these can be distressing and devastating, and they often lead to a tremendous sense of helplessness. Do not think, however, that help is unavailable. Not only do we have each other, we have centuries—millennia really—of some of the greatest minds and traditions in existence, which have laid a foundation of moral guidance for just such matters.

Judaism has always been a tradition that upholds moral behavior as the highest form of human obligation. From the TANAKH (Hebrew Bible) to the Talmud, to centuries of outstanding philosophers, legal codifiers, and mystics, Judaism offers a treasure chest of moral guidance and inspiration. In light of the extraordinary advances made in science and technology, you may think that traditional Jewish wisdom does not apply to some modern-day dilemmas. But Rabbi Elliot Dorff, an important contemporary scholar, disagrees. In his books *Matters of Life and Death, To Do the Right and the Good,* and *Love Your Neighbor and Yourself,* Rabbi Dorff presents a philosophical approach that convincingly applies Judaism's legal method to everyday moral issues and then helps us employ the principles laid out in the Jewish tradition to inform and guide us when making our own moral decisions. This study guide is a companion to Rabbi Dorff's books.

How to Use This Guide

This guide is designed for learners who wish either to begin their study of philosophy and ethics or to build on their sophistication in those areas. Its intended use is for those who are studying independently or in discussion groups, or as a supplement to a class in morality. Readers who use the guide will find it most helpful if they take the time to complete the exercises.

As noted, the primary source material for this guide is Rabbi Dorff's books. However, there are three disclaimers I would like to make for using this guide. First, although readers can use this guide on its own, a few of the exercises may prove to be difficult or impossible to complete without the background given in Rabbi Dorff's books. Therefore, I recommend that you read the appropriate sections of the books listed at the beginning of each unit when working through this guide. Second, given that this guide also supplements many biblical and rabbinic sources, it does not cover each and every topic within the three primary sources. Finally, as with Rabbi Dorff's books, this guide emphasizes the Jewish approach to moral issues. Rabbi Dorff and I trust that Judaism can guide us in answering moral questions; however, we also recognize that classical and contemporary philosophy and literary and legal theory can augment Judaism's guidance. Thus, we strongly believe that non-Jews and Jews of all denominations can use this guide as a means of challenging and advancing their own moral positions.

Objectives

The objectives for this guide are essentially twofold: after working through this book, learners will be able to identify particular moral issues and Jewish approaches regarding those issues, and they will be able to analyze and advance their own positions on those moral issues. Concerning the second objective, learners are expected to develop their own ethical reasoning. In other words, this guide expects people to state their own values, background, and understanding of morality and analyze the assumptions they are making about humanity. In this way, they can further clarify what they intuit and say about moral issues, give reasons for their positions, and articulate the fundamental beliefs that underlie their stance on specific issues. Ultimately, learners should be able to communicate the conceptual basis of their position.

The intention of this guide is not to convince people to agree with every point of Rabbi Dorff's conclusions. His books should, however, help them construct their own moral philosophy, including recognition of their assumptions and the implications of those assumptions. In this regard, they should be able to comprehend Rabbi Dorff's arguments and, if they choose to disagree, they should be able to create a reasonable argument as to why.

Journal Work

Throughout this guide, there are many questions that the learner will be asked to answer and several instances of comparative analysis. As an educator and lifelong learner, I know that there is a distinct difference between simply thinking about answers and having to explain those answers. Verbally expressing thoughts, answers, and questions—specifically by writing—forces us to refine and clarify our views. Keeping a journal is an ideal way of accomplishing such a goal, because it provides an opportunity for creating more meaning out of the study of moral philosophy.

For Your Group

For groups that are using this guide, each unit introduces activities (under the heading "For Your Group") that apply information presented in the guide or in Rabbi Dorff's books. Working in groups offers a number of options that are not available to individuals. For instance, groups provide the opportunity for cooperative learning so that people can share in, as well as challenge, each other's ideas.

Optimal group work occurs when members can provide a safe atmosphere, are able to function as a community, and are sensitive to each other's learning needs. For some of the group exercises, it may be helpful to designate roles for some individuals, such as "facilitator" and/or "recorder," so that one or two people can make sure the exercise is carried out in an organized and inclusive manner. Also, keep in mind that some of the group exercise models can be applied to other issues than the one for which it is presented; therefore, when working on any of the units, feel free to use the exercise model that seems most appropriate for your group.

- *Attention Groups:* To plan your group work, I recommend that you first check the directions for the activities before starting the unit
- *Attention Individual Learners:* Although some exercises are introduced as group work, I encourage you to look over that material—these sections often present scenarios to contemplate and exercises to complete alone and learn from

Self-Guidance

The units of this guide are intended to be independent and self-contained. In other words, no unit in this guide depends on another. Therefore, whether you are working independently or in a group, you may pick and choose the specific sections or units of the guide that appeal most to you or to your group. I encourage you to choose those sections or units that you or your group want to focus on. Certainly, however, the most thorough manner of study when using this guide is to start at the beginning and work all the way through to the end.

A Final Note

I would like to point out that Unit 1 is the most philosophically complex and abstract of all the units and is thus the longest and most difficult. Unit 2 also has a philosophical focus. You may feel perfectly comfortable beginning with these units, but if you are not used to abstract philosophy, you may prefer to begin your studies with Unit 3 (or any other unit, for that matter), which includes more concrete examples and less complex moral-reasoning exercises. Later, when you are ready, you can turn to the first two units.

Unit 1 – Introduction to Moral Philosophy: General Concepts and Theories[1]

Reading

- *Matters of Life and Death:* Appendix
- *To Do the Right and the Good:* Appendix
- *Love Your Neighbor and Yourself:* Chapter 1

Whetting Your Appetite

In July 2002, the *New York Times* reported the following case.[2]

A white couple (call them the Cohens) became parents of black twins after a mistake by a fertility clinic during in-vitro *fertilization (IVF), in what appears to be the first case of its kind in Britain. The black couple involved (call them the Smiths) sought treatment at the same clinic but could not produce any children. In* in-vitro *fertilization, which is used by tens of thousands of couples in Britain each year, sperm from the father and eggs from the mother are mixed together in the laboratory. The embryos that develop—often more than one at a time—are then placed in the mother for the nine-month period of gestation. No genetic tests are routinely carried out to ensure that the right embryos are implanted into the right woman; fertility clinics instead rely on a complex set of checks to avoid mistakes. In this case, it is unclear whether the black couple's fertilized egg was mistakenly implanted in the white woman or whether Mr. Smith's sperm had been mistakenly used to fertilize Mrs. Cohen's egg.*

Exercise

Individually or in small groups, answer the following questions, and then share your responses. If you are working alone, you may find it best to write down your initial responses and then come back to them later.

1. If the embryos were created with the Smiths' sperm and eggs, who should be considered the legal parents? Why?

2. If Mr. Smith's sperm had been mistakenly used to fertilize Mrs. Cohen's eggs, who should be considered the parents? Why?

3. In both cases, would you award any rights at all to the party whom you do *not* consider to be the parents? If so, what rights to the child would you accord and why? If not, explain.

4. Clinics do not routinely test IVF pregnancies to ensure the fetus belongs to the mother carrying it because the test is expensive and involves some risk of spontaneous abortion or injury to the child. Is that a good policy?

Life is undoubtedly filled with complexities and uncertainties. Every day we make thousands of decisions that shape the manner in which we live our lives now and direct us on our future life path. These decisions create our identity—individually, communally, nationally, and even internationally. Some solutions seem to come to us intuitively or naturally. However, some are painfully difficult and require time for reflection and research before we arrive at some resolution and peace of mind. At times, deciding the right thing to do is like driving in heavy fog with no lights.

In twenty-first-century America, life seems to have become ever more complex. This is partially due to the fact that we live in a nation of great diversity, one that spans spectra of race, ethnicity, age, religion, culture, technology, and psychology. This clearly affects our personal decisions as well as our communal dilemmas. Americans, though, hold many ideals in common, thus easing the decision-making process in many situations. In others, however, the diversity in our society makes things more difficult, offering us significantly different and/or conflicting ideals. Therefore, how do we make decisions when there are varying viewpoints to consider? How can we possibly come to conclusions about life's decisions so we feel that we have done the right thing? How can we be sure of what is right and wrong at all? Where should we look for moral or ethical guidance?

Exercise

Take a moment to answer the following questions. Write your answers in your journal.

1. Are you a moral person? If so, how?
2. What are your sources for ethical guidance?

In answering these questions, you may very well have had difficulty because of the words "ethical" and "moral." After all, what do "moral" and "ethical" mean? What are morals and ethics? What is the difference between the two? To understand what morals and ethics are, certain distinctions must first be made.

Definitions

Morals vs. Ethics

Both the word "ethics" (from Greek) and the word "morals" (from Latin) are derived from words meaning "customs." In common parlance today, there is no real difference between the two. Philosophers, however, often differentiate between the words, depending on the context. Generally, morals refer to concrete norms or standards, whereas ethics are theories about concrete norms or standards. Here is an example of a moral question: Is capital punishment right or wrong? The pertinent ethical question is: How does society have the right to determine whether capital punishment is right or wrong? In these examples, the moral question asks what the standard is and the ethical question asks the basis for the standard.

Morals vs. Customs

Customs are distinct from morals in two ways. First, customs are, by definition, not universal; customs are bound to their particular society (e.g., driving on the left or right side of the road and eating turkey rather than beef on Thanksgiving). On the other hand, morals may be universal. (Whether or not morals are universal is ultimately left to one's own philosophy, but it certainly may be argued that they are universal.) Second, given that morals focus on weightier issues than customs, violation of morals is often met with more stringent and obvious consequences than violation of customs.

Morals vs. Laws

Morals and laws differ in regard to their sources of origin. Morals come from customs, religion, culture, and reasoning. Although laws sometimes come from those same sources, they must also come from a sovereign authority. As such, they are eligible for enforcement, whereas morals are not. Also, similar to their distinction from customs, morals may be universal, but laws apply only to people who live under that particular sovereignty.

Morals vs. Religion

Clearly, morality plays a large role within religion. In fact, Thomas Jefferson believed that it is through religion that a society becomes moral, because religion sets down standards and educates

7

society about them. Religion, ultimately, is about communal bonds (from the word root "*lig,*" meaning "to connect," from which we also get the word "ligament"). Religion, by definition, can exist only within a community that is connected by adherence to certain standards. Religion addresses the interconnections among people and between people and the transcendent, imaged as God in the Western religions. Religion provides a picture of who people are and who they ought to be (prescriptions). The moral norms for the community are rooted in this picture. Secular moral philosophies discuss bonds as well, but they are usually created by one person and are not necessarily put into practice by a society.

Right vs. Good

When we speak about morals and ethics, we frequently use words such as "right," "wrong," "good," and "bad." These words help us express our points of view and make judgments; however, we rarely define these terms, for we assume that others know what we are talking about (e.g., "It was wrong for Dave to drink and drive."). Philosophers, on the other hand, often use these terms technically. Therefore, when they speak about right and wrong, they are simply talking about whether or not something is in accord with the rules or standards (that is, "right" is in accord with the rules; "wrong" is not). But when philosophers speak about good and bad, they are talking about an ideal. Thus, good and bad are statements of judgment that often require qualification (e.g., "It was bad that Dave drank and drove, because his ability was impaired and he was more likely than normal to cause an accident that could hurt someone.").

Moral Standpoints

Given these distinctions, our conception of morals and ethics may be a little clearer. It may be worthwhile at this point to reconsider these questions: Are you a moral person? What are your sources for ethical guidance? Take a moment to see if your answers are different now. Why or why not?

Regardless of whether or not your answers changed, it is hoped that you became conscious of certain personal moral assumptions. Assumptions are those ideas that we have about life, society, and purpose. They are often difficult to pinpoint, but they inform many of the decisions we make, in turn revealing what we truly believe and care about. Finally, assumptions are critical to philosophy;

because we are continually constructing our philosophies, we must be aware of such assumptions and be able to articulate them. In regard to our assumptions about morality, let us attempt to further our understanding of them by visiting a spectrum of moral standpoints.

Figure 1. Spectrum of Moral Standpoints

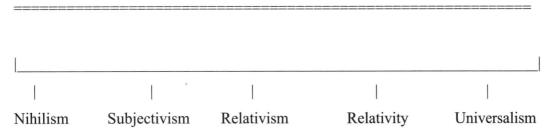

Nihilism

The word "nihilism" comes from the Latin root "*nihil,*" meaning "nothing;" this standpoint claims that there are no moral norms. Accordingly, if one thinks that something is either right or wrong, it is simply his or her opinion. This view brings to mind Thrasymachus from Plato's *The Republic,* who held that there are no concrete moral norms. All that matters is what one can be forced to do and what one can get away with. Might makes right, and so right as a moral category does not exist at all.

Subjectivism

Subjectivism is also known as the egoist standpoint. It suggests that what is good is defined by that which is good for me. Thus, each person defines morality individually, and nothing may be generalized for everyone. However, what is good for me may also be good for others.

Relativism

According to relativism, each community defines its own moral norms. Therefore, whatever a society thinks is moral is definitively moral. For example, in the United States, women may and do participate in all aspects of society. In other countries, however, it is immoral for women to appear in public. In some countries, it is perfectly moral to stand directly next to a person who is withdrawing money from an ATM; the privacy and discretion Americans deem appropriate in such circumstances are not required under all society's norms.

Relativity

Relativity, as formulated by Rabbi Dorff, suggests that there is an objective standard of morality that is universal for all, but we cannot know that standard because we are always seeing the world from only one perspective. In other words, there are universal norms—but no matter how we try to discern them, we are always seeing the world from one community, one place, and one time.

Universalism

Universalism is also known as absolutism. It maintains that moral norms are universal for all peoples in all places and that we can know them. Accordingly, if something is right in Zimbabwe it is also right in Tucson, Arizona. What is right is right and what is wrong is wrong. Period.

Exercise

Individually or with a partner, answer the following questions.

1. Define "morals."
2. What role do you think morality plays in religion?
3. What would a philosopher mean by claiming that someone was doing "the right thing" as opposed to "the good thing"?
4. How is Rabbi Dorff's moral standpoint of relativity different from relativism?
5. Which of the five moral standpoints best fits your own moral assumptions? Explain.

For Your Group

Identify with a Moral Standpoint: Exercise 1

Divide into small groups. Give each group a large piece of paper and a marker. Each group should write its responses to the following questions in big letters so that everyone can read them.

1. Of the five moral standpoints shown on the spectrum (Figure 1), which would Judaism most likely adopt? Which would the other major Western religions (Christianity and Islam) adopt?
2. Which of the moral standpoints best fits your group's moral assumptions?

After the groups have written down their answers, hang the papers on the walls of the room, arranging them according to their viewpoints. Have one person from each group act as a representative and explain the group's reasoning. Make sure to allow time for questions and answers from the other participants.

Identify with a Moral Standpoint: Exercise 2

String a real or imaginary rope across the room. Clearly identify one end as nihilism and the other as absolutism. Ask group members to find the point on the spectrum that best fits their own moral stance. Those with similar views should express their thoughts and be prepared to try to convince others to their way of thinking. After each group has given a brief presentation of its view, allow people to move to a different spot on the spectrum if they have changed their minds. Those who move should be given an opportunity to explain why.

The Theories

Aside from the spectrum of moral standpoints, an introduction to the philosophy of ethics would be incomplete without identifying the major theories and theorists in the field. These are summarized in Table 1, which also appears in *Love Your Neighbor and Yourself.*

Table 1: Moral Theories

Theory	Moral Claim	Major Theorist	Explanation
Consequentialism (whether an act is good is defined by its consequences)			
Ethical egoism	Good is that which serves one's self-interests; sometimes helping others serves this purpose	Thomas Hobbes	Although they are related, egoism as a philosophical viewpoint should not be confused with egotistical (meaning conceited)
Act utilitarianism	Good is that which is useful for the person or people in a particular situation, without taking into consideration all such situations	Jeremy Bentham	Bentham particularly focused on physical pleasure (i.e., hedonism), although the theory may be applied to other circumstances (e.g., the true story portrayed in the movie *Alive*, in which people who were stranded in the Andes ate dead humans to stay alive)
Rule utilitarianism	Good is that act which produces the most usefulness for the greatest number of people as a general rule—that is, when considering all similar situations	John Stuart Mill	Mill thought that the good must be able to be generalized to all situations and people; psychological and intellectual pleasures are just as important as physical

Deontology (there are moral principles in the very nature of things that govern us, regardless of their consequences)			
Natural law	Like physical rules (e.g., gravity), moral rules are built into the structure of nature	Thomas Aquinas	The lists of such moral rules vary in accordance with each natural law theorist
Kantian ethics	Moral rules can be generated from the mind because the mind has a logical structure	Immanuel Kant	Kant has two versions of his categorical imperative: Do only that which can be generalized to others and never treat people merely as a means
Ross's theory of ethics	There are seven moral principles that all people have the duty to fulfill (e.g., keeping promises and being truthful)	W. D. Ross	Ross claims that moral situations are complex and that people have intuitive moral duties for one another; thus, when moral duties conflict, one must balance the fulfillment of those duties
Theological ethics	God defines what is good and bad	Western religious theorists	God's will is usually derived from the literature that the theorist deems to be a true revelation or prophesy

Virtue or character ethics (a person deemed moral or worthy of setting values defines what is good)			
Moral perfection	The moral champion, who strives for moral perfection, is the ideal	Prophets; Book of Psalms	
Wisdom; success in life	The person who succeeds in life because of vast life experience is the moral authority	Books of Proverbs and Ecclesiastes	
Combining the ideal and real	The person who embodies moral qualities or virtues in concrete life situations is the moral authority	Aristotle; the Rabbis	
The powerful noble man	The noble person (one who creates his or her own values as opposed to being subservient to others' values) is the moral authority	Friedrich Nietzsche	
Feminist ethics	The morally ideal person thinks of men and women as equals	Betty Friedan, Gloria Steinam, Judith Plaskow	Traditionally, women have had ideas and solutions for moral issues that were ignored; therefore, ethics must be rethought with a view to correcting whatever male bias it may contain

For Your Group

The Informational Jigsaw Puzzle

For this exercise, each person in the group will be both a teacher and a learner. You can work individually or in pairs.

1. Assign a philosophical theory to each person, pair, or group.

2. Each group should take five to eight minutes to get acquainted with the theory well enough to be able to explain it to another person or group.

3. During those five to eight minutes, the group takes three pieces of paper and writes a question and its answer on each piece. The answers should reflect and identify the theory the group represents.

4. Collect all of the questions and mix them up so they are in random order; put them aside for later.

5. Form new pairs or groups. Each new group should have a representative member for all of the assigned theories. Allow three to five minutes for each person to explain the theory he or she just learned, or until each representative has had the opportunity to speak. (This should take approximately fifteen to twenty minutes total.)

6. Finally, the facilitator reads to the whole group the questions that were put aside earlier and solicits answers from all but those who wrote the specific questions. This can also be done on a point system.[3]

Note: The Informational Jigsaw Puzzle model can also be used with the Spectrum of Moral Standpoints (Fig. 1). Instead of assigning each group a philosophical theory, each explores a moral standpoint.

Follow-Up Questions

Using Table 1, answer the following questions. Either write the answers in your journal or discuss possible answers with the group.

1. What is the difference between act utilitarianism and rule utilitarianism?

2. One example of the morality of act utilitarianism is provided in the table. What is another example that would be considered moral under act utilitarianism but not under rule utilitarianism?

3. The second version of Kant's categorical imperative is to not treat people merely as a means. Can you explain this? Feel free to use an example.

4. Do you agree with the moral claim posed by the feminist ethics? Why or why not?

5. Of the several ethical theories and subsets presented, which best fits your own theory of morality? Explain.

6. Based on your answer to question 3, can you identify your moral assumptions and the implications of those assumptions? For example: "Because I agree with Kant, my assumptions are that logical reasoning is the primary source of morality. Therefore, along with taking into account the categorical imperative, one must think critically and logically about the situation and base a moral decision on logical conclusions."

Recommended Reading for Unit 1

Arthur, John, ed. *Morality and Moral Controversies: Readings in Moral, Social, and Political Philosophy* (Upper Saddle River, NJ: Prentice Hall, 2002).

Denise, Theodore C., Sheldon P. Peterfreund, and Nicholas P. White, eds. *Great Traditions in Ethics (*Belmont, CA: Wadsworth, 1996).

Moore, Brooke N., and Robert M. Stewart, eds. *Moral Philosophy: A Comprehensive Introduction* (Mountain View, CA: Mayfield, 1994).

Unit 2 – Judaism's Methodology and Moral Course of Action

Reading

- *Matters of Life and Death:* Appendix; pp. 267–270 (Optional)
- *To Do the Right and the Good:* Chapter 1; Appendix B
- *Love Your Neighbor and Yourself:* Chapter 1; Appendix

North Americans are familiar with three primary ideologies for determining what is right and good, each with its own benefits and pitfalls: Catholicism, Protestantism, and American secularism. Catholicism depends on its clergy and on the pope (the highest clerical authority) to define what is right and good. Whether or not they agree with the pope, Catholics understand that when he defines a matter of morals (or of faith), it is infallibly decided. Protestants stress the importance of using one's individual conscience to define what is right and good. Protestant morality is guided by Scripture (Christian Bible)—in particular, the stories of Jesus—and the principles and practices upheld by the various denominations. American secularism, which is deeply influenced by both Protestantism and Enlightenment thought, maintains trust in both individual conscience and in rule by the majority in a government with distributed powers. As Rabbi Dorff points out:

American secular ideology . . . sees us, first, as isolated individuals endowed by our Creator (whether that be God or Nature) with "certain unalienable Rights, and among these are Life, Liberty, and the pursuit of Happiness." We may choose to give up some of those rights to gain benefits of communities and governments, but the ultimate truth is that we are individuals with rights first and citizens with duties second.[4]

Although American Jews have been influenced by these ideologies (for example, in Reform Judaism, which, like American ideology, stresses the role of individual choice in deciding when and how to live by tradition), the Jewish tradition uses *halakhah* (Jewish law) and a legal approach to determine morality. *Halakhah,* originating in the Torah, is determined by rabbis whose interpretations and rulings appear in various books of law (e.g., the Talmud and legal codes such as Maimonides' *Mishneh Torah* and Yosef Karo's *Shulchan Arukh*). These books provide the prescriptions for how a Jew should behave morally. In Judaism, moral laws have at least as much authority as rituals do.

You Be the Rabbi[5]

Individually or in small groups, read the following scenario. Then, using the Jewish source material listed below, determine how an Orthodox rabbi, a Reform rabbi, and a Conservative rabbi might respond to this halakhic and moral dilemma. Be sure to explain what line of reasoning these rabbis would use to justify their responses.

Scenario

Sarah is an eighteen-year-old Jewish freshman at Pepperdine University. Several of Sarah's friends, both Jewish and non-Jewish, have tattoos, with designs ranging from crucifixes to Bugs Bunny's face. Sarah has often thought how cool it would be to have a tattoo of something meaningful—maybe on her shoulder or ankle (somewhere inconspicuous)—but she is not only unsure of what tattoo would best permanently represent herself, she is afraid of how her family will react. Sarah's parents are against tattooing because they believe that tattoos disgrace the human form, but Sarah's friends say that she has to do what she believes is best. Sarah does not know what to do. On the one hand, Sarah believes that people were given their bodies for a certain reason, but, on the other hand, she believes anything is okay as long as it does not hurt others.

Jewish Source Material

- "And God created man in His image, in the image of God He created him; male and female He created them" (Gen. 1:27).[6]
- "Mark, the heavens to their uttermost reaches belong to the Lord your God, the earth and all that is on it" (Deut. 10:14).
- "You shall not make gashes in your flesh for the dead, nor incise any marks on yourselves: I am the Lord" (Lev. 19:28).
- "The Holy Blessed One brings the soul and throws it into the body and judges them as one" (B. *Sanhedrin* 91b).
- "If a man wrote [on his skin] pricked in writing [he is culpable for punishment (i.e., flogging)] . . . but only if he writes it and pricks it in with ink or eye-paint or anything that leaves a lasting mark. Rabbi Simeon b. Judah says in the name of Rabbi Simeon: 'He

16

is not culpable unless he writes there the name [of a god], for it is written, *Nor incise any marks upon yourselves: I am the Lord*'" (M. *Makkot* 3:6).

- "[Tattooing] was a custom among pagans who marked themselves for idolatry" (Maimonides, *Laws of the Worship of Stars and the Statutes of the Idolators,* 12:11).[7]

- Aaron Demsky of Bar Ilan University suggests that non-idolatrous tattooing was permitted in biblical times by the following references: "One shall say, 'I am the Lord's,' another shall use the name of 'Jacob,' another shall mark his arm, 'of the Lord' and adopt the name of 'Israel'" (Isa. 44:5) and "Is as a sign on every man's hand, that all men know His doings" (Job 37:7).

How do you think each of the three rabbis would deal with Sarah's situation?

Now that you have predicted the rabbis' responses, it is noteworthy to mention that there are Jews who believe tattooing is against Jewish law (Orthodox and some Conservative) and therefore bar Jews with tattoos from participating in Jewish ritual life, positions of honor, and from being buried in a Jewish cemetery. Rabbi Dorff does not believe that the tradition supports this point of view and thinks that those with non-idolatrous tattoos should not be barred from any of those Jewish ritual elements.[8] Rabbi Dorff concurs with the responsum (rabbinic ruling) adopted in 1997 by the Committee on Jewish Laws and Standards (CJLS) of the Conservative Movement, submitted by Rabbi Alan B. Lucas, which concludes that although tattooing should be discouraged because it is a violation of the Torah, those who have tattoos may practice fully in Jewish ritual life and may be buried in a Jewish cemetery.

Journal Work: Reflection
Answer the following questions. If you would like, share your answers with a partner.

1. Describe the experience of using a legal approach to solving a moral dilemma. Did it make solving the dilemma harder? Easier? Was it forced for you or did it come naturally?
2. Do you believe that one could come to a good solution through this method? Why or why not?

For Your Group

Role-Playing

Create scenes to role-play using the scenario presented earlier in this unit. Divide into groups of twos, threes, or fours. Assign each person a role. Here are some suggested roles:

- *Sarah:* Here is some additional information about Sarah. She comes from an upper-middle class family that lives in Encino, California. Sarah was very popular in high school and is outgoing. She says that she is a spiritual person, but she has never completely identified with her Judaism.

- *Vicki:* Vicki is Sarah's best friend at Pepperdine. She is not Jewish and does not respect religion because it makes people feel guilty about doing what they want to do. Last year, Vicki got a tattoo of a small dolphin on her shoulder; she says it represents power, grace, and freedom.

- *Ted:* Ted is a devout member of the Church of Christ and is one of Sarah's and Vicki's friends at Pepperdine. Ted is not pushy about his passionate Christian beliefs but he does not like the idea that Sarah is contemplating a tattoo. He believes that it is a sin to do things for the beautification of the body, because the body houses the impulse for sin.

- *Laura:* Laura is Sarah's mother. She was brought up in a Conservative Jewish household and likes Jewish culture. Laura has worked as an elementary school teacher most of her life and wants Sarah to become a doctor or a lawyer. Laura is very concerned with outward appearances and would not want Sarah to do anything that might make others disrespect her and lessen her career or life opportunities.

- *David:* David, Sarah's father, was brought up in an Orthodox Jewish home. When he left to go to Yale for college, he stopped practicing Orthodoxy and turned to the Conservative movement. He is more religious and observant than Laura, but they respect each other deeply. Although some Conservative Jews have tattoos, David does not condone them himself. David is still angry that Sarah chose to attend an outwardly Christian university.

Feel free to embellish or change any of these characters or to add more characters.

Each group should prepare a three- to five-minute skit portraying a possible, realistic, interaction concerning Sarah's choice about getting a tattoo. The groups should try to develop the characters' positions on the subject while working to come to a solution to Sarah's dilemma. After each group has presented its skit, the entire group discusses and critiques the interactions among the characters, the problems raised, and the conclusions.

Present a Position

For this exercise, divide into three to five small groups. Assign each group one of the viewpoints listed below. Each group should devise a solution to Sarah's dilemma based on the perspective of its assigned viewpoint.

- Group 1: Reform Judaism
- Group 2: Conservative Judaism
- Group 3: Orthodox Judaism
- Group 4: Protestantism (if needed)
- Group 5: American secularism (if needed)

Groups 4 and 5 may need to consult the readings in *To Do the Right and the Good* (listed at the beginning of the unit) for help in developing their positions.

After all the groups present their positions on tattooing, review each perspective, highlighting its strengths and weaknesses in regard to Sarah's moral problem.

Questions and Answers

Write short answers to the following questions and then read the possible answers. After you have completed this section, you may want to review the predictions you made about the rabbis' responses to Sarah's dilemma.

Question: What are the potential pitfalls of a legal approach to morality?

Possible answers: Rabbi Dorff points out three potential problems that a legal approach may create:

- Some people may act in accordance with the law as an end rather than a means. Such people become "religious behaviorists," doing what they are required to do but remaining blind to the phenomena and meanings the law was intended to reveal.
- Some people concern themselves with the details to the exclusion of the broader aims and spirit of the law (they are "legalistic") rather than appropriately using the legal approach, by which the views and spirit of the law shape one's perspective of the details.
- Some people become overly conservative and fearful of changing the law. Conserving the law can be a benefit, because it ensures continuity; but if people are too conservative, moral thinking and action can lag behind contemporary moral sensitivities and become downright reactionary in some areas.

Question: What are the possible benefits of a legal approach to morality?

Possible answers: Rabbi Dorff presents eight advantages of Judaism's linking matters of conscience to the spirit of the law, each of which is explained in full in the readings for this unit.

- Law establishes minimum moral standards with the understanding that they are not the full extent of how one needs to extend himself or herself to others.
- Law gives moral values and ideals concrete application and reality.
- Law defines the requirements and the limits of moral demands, keeping people from doing too little or too much.
- Law provides a public forum for adjudicating moral conflicts.
- Law, properly interpreted and applied, affords continuity and flexibility, balancing the need to maintain tradition with the need to accommodate changes.
- Law provides one important way to teach morality.
- Law preserves the integrity of moral intentions, because it tests the nature and seriousness of our intentions so that we may avoid hypocrisy, and it brings our intentions into the realm of action, where we can see them clearly.
- Law contributes to creating a moral community by specifying the behavior required of people to make justice a living value in society.

Almost all rabbis and Jews would probably agree with each of these eight advantages to a legal approach. It is interesting, however, that the fifth item (balancing tradition with change) may raise some eyebrows and possibly generate disapproval from Orthodox Jews, not necessarily because of what it says but because of how it may be interpreted. Jews, primarily influenced by their denomination, disagree strongly on how to maintain the balance between tradition and change. They argue about who determines when it is acceptable to make a change, about who has the authority to initiate a change, and about the implications of making a change.

Generally speaking, Orthodox Jews believe that the Torah—both written and oral traditions—consists of the exact words of God. Accordingly, humans do not have the authority to change laws and ideas, because God revealed the answers to all future questions at Mount Sinai, and humans do not know more than God. Therefore, in regard to legal decisions, Orthodox Jews are primarily concerned with which traditional position in the codes or response to apply to any given situation.

Reform Jews, in distinct opposition to the Orthodox, believe that the Torah portrays God's will in moral laws but was written by human beings and, as time goes on, we begin to understand God's will better and better (Progressive Revelation). For that reason, even though they may consult the Jewish tradition, Reform Jews believe that the traditional laws have no authority in our time and that every individual should be able to decide what aspects of God's will to obey and how to do so. In addition, Reform Jews will take modern-day morality and historical circumstances into strong consideration when making decisions.

Conservative Jews assert a variety of ideological standpoints that lie between the Orthodox and the Reform movements and that are, therefore, difficult to define precisely. Overall, Conservative Jews believe that the Torah has both some sort of divine status and some sort of human influence. The Torah is definitely a record of God's will, but the laws can be interpreted and applied anew by rabbis and, for some, must be reinterpreted, because each generation experiences a new form of divine revelation and the laws must stay viable to the members of the community (Continuous Revelation). Thus, Conservative Jews will strongly consult the Jewish tradition yet not discount contemporary morality and historical circumstances in their decisions.[9]

Summary

This unit and its exercises are designed to help you become more familiar with the methodology of the Jewish approach to moral issues. As you can see from Sarah's story, there are a number of ways of deriving solutions for her dilemma from the Jewish sources presented. The specific solution reached largely depends on one's philosophical and theological assumptions about the Torah, humanity, responsibility to one's own body and modesty, and responsibility to one's parents. The implication of those assumptions determines whether you—and Sarah—believe it is acceptable for someone to have a tattoo.

For Jews, thinking about these issues requires building a web of reasoning with law, theology, stories, and other traditional Jewish sources; contemporary sociology, psychology, and history; and a little good, old-fashioned intuition. For American Jews, American perspectives and values will also play a role. For Catholics, Protestants, and American secularists, the web would surely be constructed differently. We will later revisit some of the aspects of moral philosophy that we dealt with in this unit, but in the meantime, what elements make up the web of your reasoning when facing a moral issue?

Recommended Reading for Unit 2

Cytron, Barry D., and Earl Schwartz, eds. *When Life Is in the Balance: Life and Death Decisions in Light of the Jewish Tradition* (New York: United Synagogue Youth, 1986).

Dorff, Elliot N., and Louis E. Newman, eds. *Contemporary Jewish Ethics and Morality* (New York: Oxford University Press, 1995).

Herring, Basil F. *Jewish Ethics and Halakhah for Our Time: Sources and Commentary* (New York: KTAV and Yeshiva University Press, 1984).

Klein, Isaac. *A Guide to Jewish Religious Practice.* (New York: Jewish Theological Seminary of America, 1979).

Unit 3 – Our Bodies: What Are We Responsible For?

Readings

- *Matters of Life and Death:* Chapter 2; 10
- *Love Your Neighbor and Yourself:* Appendix

In his Pulitzer Prize-winning work *The Denial of Death,* Ernest Becker points out that human beings are caught in a paradoxical dilemma over their physical essence: On the one hand, human beings all have an awareness of their "own splendid uniqueness," and on the other, they have an awareness that they are flawed, fated to go "back into the ground a few feet in order to blindly and dumbly rot."[10] Although some believe that morality plays a role only when relating to others, Becker shows that our own psyche—and, I would add, our own spirit—has an awareness and relationship to our bodies, which leads to issues and questions regarding our moral assumptions. Such questions are: Why should I feel responsible for my own body if I am only destined to rot forever? Why do I feel special and unique in regard to my body? What exactly am I responsible for in regard to my own body? What are the implications of such responsibilities for my life?

Considering the theories of ethics in general literature presented in Unit 1, several answers to these questions may be offered. First, one might claim that acting responsibly toward our bodies makes us feel good (i.e., being healthy feels good); therefore, it is our moral responsibility to treat our bodies well. Second, one might claim that we can never view ourselves as wholly separate from other people, and even if we are doing something that affects only our own bodies, it could still have ramifications for others. Therefore, as an intuitive duty and responsibility to others, we have the moral obligation to act responsibly with our own bodies. And, third, one might note that people who embody moral qualities and virtues act responsibly toward their own bodies; thus, we, too, should act responsibly toward our bodies if we want to be moral.

Journal Work: Exploring Assumptions

Write short answers to the following questions. Feel free to share your answers with others.

1. Do you act responsibly toward your own body (e.g., do you maintain your health)? Why or why not? What is your line of reasoning?

2. Do you knowingly do things that may cause your body harm? How do you justify this?

Duty to Act Responsibly

Judaism teaches that we have moral responsibilities both to others and to God. We have a duty to God to care for our bodies. In fact, one of the most important mitzvot (commandments or legal obligations) is to preserve physical life (*pikuakh nefesh*). *Pikuakh nefesh,* as Rabbi Dorff explains, takes precedence over all other commandments except for murder, idolatry, and incestuous or adulterous sexual intercourse.

Rabbi Dorff created seven tenets that he claims affirm Judaism's reasoning for why we should act responsibly toward our bodies.[11]

1. The body belongs to God. The Torah teaches that God owns everything in the universe, including our bodies (see Exod. 19:5; Deut. 10:14; Ps. 24:1). Consequently, men and women do not have the right to govern their bodies as they will; because God created our bodies and owns them, God can and does assert the right to restrict how we use our bodies according to the rules articulated in Jewish law.

2. Human worth stems from being created in God's image. Moral prescriptions come from our ability to distinguish good from bad and right from wrong (the basis of moral knowledge); to speak; and, at least partially, to share in God's spiritual nature.

3. The human being is an integrated whole. Although some Jewish thinkers have been influenced by the Gnostic and Christian ideas of bifurcation of the body and soul, by and large the Jewish tradition teaches that they are inseparable and one is not necessarily superior to the other.

4. The body is morally neutral and potentially good. The body should be used within the framework of holiness delineated by Jewish law and theology. That holiness is not attained by depriving ourselves of physical pleasures nor by enduring pain but rather by using all our faculties, including our bodily energies.

5. Jews have a mandate and duty to pursue healing. Jews are under the divine imperative to help God preserve and protect what is God's, including using medicine and medical care (derived, in the Talmud, from Exod. 21:19-20), aiding another in a life-threatening situation (B. *Sanhedrin* 73a), and living in a community where there is a physician (J. *Kiddushin* 66d; B. *Sanhedrin* 17b).

6. The community must balance its medical and non-medical needs and services. Not only do the individuals and the physician have the duty to heal, but the community is charged with providing the necessities that preserve life and Jewish living.

7. Jews must sanctify God's name. The Torah demands that our actions and words bring honor to our community; to God, to whom we dedicate ourselves; and to ourselves.

Exercise

Individually or with a partner, match the following statements with the tenet (listed above) they best represent. Be able to explain why you made your matches.

A. In the end, my body and spirit are seen as one.

B. Every city where Jews live must have some sort of public health measures, such as public water and sewage systems.

C. I am grateful for the life that I have been given, and I must do what I can to preserve it.

D. Desecrating myself would be an affront to myself and to all Jews.

E. The body is an amazing vehicle with which to experience many of life's wonders.

F. Each person has the power to affect the world through what he or she says and does, and one must use that power for good rather than for bad.

G. We are partners with God in the ongoing act of creation.

You Make the Call

Individually or with a partner, read the following moral dilemma concerning our responsibility to our bodies. Then answer the question that follows.

Scenario

Currently, the National Football League, the National Basketball Association, and International Olympic Committee test their athletes for steroids, but the Major League Baseball does not.

Steroids elevate the body's testosterone level, increasing muscle mass; this effect is greatly enhanced when the drugs are taken in conjunction with proper nutrition and strength training. Steroid use can increase an athlete's physical capabilities and concentration. In a *Sports Illustrated* article from 2002,[12] Ken Caminiti (the 1996 Most Valuable Player) admitted to using steroids and claimed that 50 percent of Major League players also use them. Steroid use may be the cause of the greatest extended slugging era that baseball has ever seen, with players shattering team and league home run records. In addition to being illegal in the United States, steroids have side effects, including heart and liver damage, persistent endocrine system imbalance, elevated cholesterol levels, susceptibility to strokes, aggressive behavior, and sexual dysfunction. Current Major League players have denied that there are as many steroid users as Caminiti suggests; most have said 20 to 30 percent of players take the drugs. The players are divided on whether the league should test for steroids with the purpose of banning their use.

Do you think Major League Baseball should introduce testing for steroids? Explain your answer and define the assumptions you are making about morality and our responsibilities to our bodies.

For Your Group

The Debate

Divide into two to four groups. Assign one of the following viewpoints of the steroid debate to each group.

- Group 1: The Association of Baseball Owners (including the commissioner)—for testing
- Group 2: The Players Association—against testing
- Group 3: A select committee of fans (if needed)—some are for testing (steroids are illegal and unfairly skew the game) and others are against testing (the increase in home runs and aggressive play are good for the fans)
- Group 4: A nonbiased panel of experts in morality (if needed)—employed to lend insight, rationale, and possible solutions

After each group has had time to prepare its points and counterpoints, conduct a debate of this issue. It may be helpful to assign a "debate facilitator" in order to organize and arrange the debate.

Summary

How we understand our responsibilities toward our bodies has great significance in many of our decisions. This understanding may not only affect us physically, psychologically, and spiritually but may affect others as well, including family, friends, and the greater community. A large part of the moral issue over our own bodies revolves around our individual freedom and rights; however, our moral assumptions regarding freedom and rights do not always coincide with other people's moral assumptions, especially concerning the setting of policies and laws. Judaism teaches us to see our bodies in a deeply meaningful way, and this leads to important responsibilities. In the units that follow, some of the implications for Judaism's view of the body and the responsibilities we have for our own body are discussed.

Recommended Reading for Unit 3

Howard Eilberg-Schwartz, ed. *People of the Body: Jews and Judaism from an Embodied Perspective (Suny Series, the body in culture, history, and religion)* (New York: State University of New York, 1992).

Blume, Sheila B., and Stephen J. Levy, eds. *Addictions in the Jewish Community* (New York: Commission on Synagogue Relations of the Federations of Jewish Philanthropies of New York, 1986).

Novick, Bernard. *In God's Image: Making Jewish Decisions about the Body* (New York: United Synagogue of America, 1980).

Waskow, Arthur. *Down-to-Earth Judaism: Food, Money, Sex, and the Rest of Life* (New York: William Morrow, 1995).

Unit 4 – Sexual Morality

Readings

- *Matters of Life and Death:* Chapter 5
- *Love Your Neighbor and Yourself:* Chapter 3

Sex is an enormous issue in American society and it directly relates to how we understand our responsibilities to our own and others' bodies. The media have a significant influence on our views because they are saturated with sexuality. As conduits of pop culture, television, magazines, and the music industry use sexual appeal as a means of attracting consumers. Sexual appeal and activities are portrayed as extremely important and desirable, perhaps even the most crucial aspects of one's personal and public identity.

The topic of sex and the media surely raises its own subset of moral concerns. In addition, many other sexually related issues are raised, including societal problems in regard to sexual promiscuity and infidelity, teen pregnancy, and sexually transmitted diseases. American society's views on sex cover the spectrum from complete sexual liberation and freedom to rigid restraint of sexual expression that limits sex solely to procreation.

The Jewish tradition has always understood sex to have two primary purposes: procreation and marital companionship. Accordingly, sex is a deeply meaningful act, which is not exclusively physical. As Rabbi Dorff eloquently states:

> *Even if two people verbally declare to each other that their sex act is only for physical pleasure with no intention of further commitments, what they are conveying with their bodies belies what they have said with their lips. Such a situation, in other words, is rife with the potential for miscommunication, misunderstood intentions, and deeply hurt feelings. Undoubtedly, that is one reason that the Jewish tradition wants sex to be restricted to marriage.[13]*

Thus, considering the significance of the sex act, the Jewish tradition emphasizes that the married couple be loving friends (*re'im ahuvim*). Furthermore, the sex act has the potential of procreation, which adds another reason to restrict it to marriage. Children not only are a blessing as both our heritage and our destiny but impose a tremendous responsibility for us to raise and educate them.

Although Judaism posits that marriage is the most appropriate context for sexual intercourse, it certainly happens outside of marriage. However, not completely living up to the Jewish ideal does not free Jews from incorporating as much of the ideal as possible into their lives; morality does not occur within a paradigm of all or nothing. That is, even in a non-marital sexual relationship, moral principles must be applied.

Conceptual Awareness

Read the following exemples and a) put them in order of most moral to least moral and b) identify the moral principle or principles (as many as you can) that are either upheld or broken in each one. Please note: there is no one "correct" order. Put the following scenarios on cards. Divide into groups and follow the instructions above.

Scenarios

- Joe and Lauren are highly attracted to each other physically. One of them is usually spending the night at the other one's apartment, even though they rarely see each other in the daytime. Lauren's roommate, Amber, feels put upon because the couple is always "all over each other." Joe and Lauren have no regard for Amber's presence. Furthermore, Joe and Lauren are never really interested in talking to each other, neither sharing their own lives nor learning about each other's, so most of their time together is spent engaged in sexual activities.

- No matter how Josh is feeling, he always takes time to listen to Nicole so that he can be aware of her feelings and mood. Sometimes he feels very sexual, but he would never force or impose his will on Nicole because he appreciates the fact that she may not feel the same.

- Matthew and Ariella have been sexually active together for a few months. When Ariella goes out to parties and clubs without Matthew, she often leads people to believe that she is not committed to anyone. She has never told Matthew that she does this. Since she has been with Matthew, however, she has not had sex with anyone else.

- Brian and Jessica have been seeing each other and have been sexually active for six months. Brian works out at the gym every other day at the same time. An employee at the gym whom Brian finds very attractive has been flirting with him for two weeks. Finally, the employee asks Brian out for a date. He tells her that he is flattered but he is already involved with someone else.

- Donny and Jennifer have been dating for three weeks. Lately, when they kiss it is becoming more and more passionate, and both of them realize that they are bound to have sex soon. Therefore, in as tactful and compassionate a manner as he could, Donny told Jennifer about his sexual history and asked her about hers. He also told her that he is very sexually attracted to her, but he wants to get an HIV test first and hopes that she will come with him and get one too.

- Geoffrey and Elana have been sexually active for some time, and they now are about to have sex once again. However, this time they both stop for a moment because they realize that neither of them has a condom. Knowing for sure that they are both healthy, and being caught up in their passion and lust, they continue what they are doing and have sex.

- Isaac attends a large university where there are a lot of attractive women. Christie, a young woman in his economics class, frequently sits next to him and finally asks Isaac to go to a movie. Isaac goes with her, and after the movie he tells Christie that he is Jewish. Christie, an Episcopalian, says that Isaac's religion does not matter to her. However, Isaac apologizes and tells Christie that his Judaism is very important to him and he cannot date non-Jews.

These scenarios are meant to clarify the eight primary Jewish principles informing the use of our bodies. In the readings for this unit, Rabbi Dorff outlines the principles governing a non-marital sexual relationship:

- Seeing oneself and one's partner as distinctly human creatures of God, created in the divine image
- Respect for others
- Modesty
- Honesty
- Fidelity

- Health and safety
- The possibility of a child
- The Jewish quality of the relationship

The last one is especially noteworthy because divorce rates are double for mixed-religion couples, and 90 percent of children from these couples are not raised Jewish.

As you can see, upholding these principles in a non-marital relationship may be difficult, but, nevertheless, it is possible for those who are mature, committed, and striving to create and maintain a relationship to embody a measure of morality that approaches what is experienced in marriage.

Journal Work: Reflection

Answer the following questions. Feel free to share your answers with others.

1. Is Rabbi Dorff's list of moral principles for a non-marital sexual relationship a good one? Are there any principles that should not be included or are missing? If so, which?
2. Do you think that moral principles should govern a sexual relationship, or do you think that people should do whatever they want? Why? In either case, what moral assumptions are you making about humanity? About the purposes of sex?

For Your Group

Integrating the Concepts

Review Rabbi Dorff's eight moral principles for a non-marital sexual relationship.

- The group's recorder or facilitator should have several small pieces of paper (one for each member of the group); he or she writes one of the principles on each piece of paper, making sure that all eight are used.
- Randomly distribute the papers to each member.
- Each member then creates an illustrative scenario to exemplify the principle he or she was given.
- After everyone has finished, the examples are read to the entire group. The members then guess which principle is demonstrated by each scenario.

31

Summary

Clearly, for Judaism, sex is designated for the married couple because marriage is seen as a sanctified and separate relationship in which this special form of intimacy should happen. Although sex is for procreation, it is also for marital companionship. In fact, the Torah and the Rabbis of the Talmud understood that both partners have sexual appetites that need to be satisfied for the sake of marital companionship, even in times during and after child rearing.

Obviously, however, people engage in sex outside of marriage. Judaism sees sex as a profoundly sacred act; after all, this act has the potential and power to create life. Sex is also the most physically intimate that two people can be with each other, and it has significant emotional implications for that relationship. For these reasons, Judaism has moral values and principles that apply to a sexual relationship, both in and out of marriage. These principles are valuable not just for the sake of respecting one's partner but also for respecting one's relationship with God and with oneself.

Related Topics

- Masturbation
- Contraception

Recommended Reading for Unit 4

Borowitz, Eugene. *Choosing a Sex Ethic: A Jewish Enquiry* (New York: Schocken, 1969).

Gordis, Robert. *Love and Sex: A Modern Jewish Perspective* (New York: Farrar Strauss Giroux, 1978).

Grossman, Susan, and Rivka Haut. *Daughters of the King* (Philadelphia: Jewish Publication Society, 1992).

Kramer, David. *The Jewish Family: Metaphor and Memory* (New York: Oxford University Press, 1989).

Silverstein, Alan. *It All Begins with a Date: Jewish Concerns about Intermarriage* (Northvale, NJ: Aronson, 1995).

Unit 5 – Abortion

Readings

- *Matters of Life and Death:* Chapter 5 (esp. pp. 128–133)
- *Love Your Neighbor and Yourself:* Chapter 3 (esp. pp. 252–257)

Abortion has been a controversial topic in the United States for the past several decades. The debate has entered the realm of politics; has been the subject of protests; and has even led to threats, vandalism, and violence. Most of the antiabortion rhetoric and action have come from the influence of classic Christianity's stance on abortion.

Catholics and fundamentalist Protestants have two significant problems with abortion. First, they believe that at conception each individual soul inherits the taint of its primordial ancestors (Original Sin); therefore, the fetus must be born so the child can be baptized. Otherwise, the soul is condemned to death in the heavenly world as well as in this one, making abortion worse than murder. The second stems from the Septuagint (the third-century B.C.E. Greek translation of the Hebrew Bible). The modern translation of Exod. 21:22–23 follows:

> *When men fight and one of them pushes a pregnant woman and a miscarriage results, but no other damage ensues, the one responsible shall be fined according as the woman's husband may exact from him, the payment to be based on reckoning. But if other damage ensues, the penalty shall be life for life.*

The Hebrew word in question is "*ason,*" meaning "damage." However, the Septuagint rendered the word "*ason*" as "form," which is understood to be referring to an embryo or fetus. Thus, verse 23 is interpreted in classic Christianity as prescribing the death penalty for one who causes a miscarriage or abortion.

Although Judaism absolutely has a bias toward preserving life, it does not have the two problems posed by classic Christianity. Therefore, it permits abortion in some cases and actually requires it in others. This being said, Jewish law definitely prefers the use of birth control that prevents conception in the first place and, accordingly, notes that abortion may never be used as a post facto form of birth control.

Journal Work: Exploring Assumptions

Write short answers to the following questions. Feel free to share your answers with a partner.

1. Do you believe that it is ever okay for a woman to have an abortion?
2. What are you assuming about the nature of the fetus?
3. What are you assuming about the rights and responsibilities of the mother (or parents)?
4. What are the criteria for an acceptable abortion (e.g., length of pregnancy, relationship of the parents, health concerns)?

Some Facts

Approximately 3,900,000 children are born each year in the United States,[14] and it is estimated that between 20 and 30 percent of all pregnancies in this country end in abortion.[15] In 1973, the U.S. Supreme Court ruled, in *Roe v. Wade,* that it is a constitutional right for a woman to have an abortion, based on her right to privacy.[16] Today, there are more than 1 million intentional or induced abortions performed each year.[17] The reasons most often cited for having an abortion are the following:

- The pregnancy threatens the life of the mother
- The pregnancy may seriously damage the mother's physical health
- The pregnancy may seriously damage the mother's mental health
- The pregnancy threatens the economic well-being of the mother (and family)
- It is likely that the fetus has a severe defect
- The pregnancy is the result of rape or incest
- The pregnancy violates the woman's or the couple's family planning objectives (do not want to have children at all; do not want to have a child at this time; do not want to have a child with this partner)
- The mother is a minor with no family support or resources for raising a child

Ethicists debate which, if any, of these cited reasons are worthy of abortion. Much of the debate is over personhood—that is, the status and rights of the fetus.

A Jewish Approach

Part of the reason that Judaism finds abortion permissible is because it does not understand the fetus to be a person. The Talmud (B. *Yevamot* 69b) claims that within the first forty days of conception, the fetus is "simply water." It also notes (B. *Hullin* 58a) that the fetus is legally categorized as being "like the thigh of its mother" and does not attain the full rights and protections of an independent human being until birth. However, because our bodies are God's property (see Unit 3), we are not allowed to amputate, except to preserve life, so abortion is mostly forbidden as an act of self-injury—not as an act of murder.

In the readings for this unit, Rabbi Dorff says, "Jewish law requires abortion when the mother's health—physical or mental—is threatened by the pregnancy; Jewish law permits abortion when the risk to the woman's life or health (again physical or mental) is greater than that of a normal pregnancy but not so great as to constitute a clear and present danger to her." This ruling is based primarily on interpretations of the following two sources:

If a woman has [life-threatening] difficulty in childbirth, one dismembers the embryo in her, limb by limb, because her life takes precedence over its life. Once its head [or its "greater part"] has emerged, it may not be touched, for we do not set aside one life for another (M. Ohalot 7:6).

This, too, is a negative commandment: one must not take pity on the life of a pursuer (rodef). And so the sages taught: "If a woman has [life-threatening] difficulty in childbirth," it is permitted to dismember the fetus in her abdomen, either by a medication or by hand, for it is like a rodef who is pursuing to kill her. But from the moment his head emerges he is not to be touched, "for we do not set aside one life for another," for this is the natural course of things (M.T. Laws of a Murderer 1:9).

The questions, however, that still remain are: How much of a threat to a woman's life must the fetus pose to justify or require an abortion? What exactly constitutes physical and mental health?

You Be the Judge

Individually or in small groups, read the following scenarios and decide whether the abortion was justifiable.

Scenario 1

Ann and Bernie were a financially secure, socially well-established couple in their mid-forties. The success of Bernie's business gave him great satisfaction and allowed the couple to freely pursue its various social and recreational interests. Their two children were both in their twenties and had lived away from home for several years. At this point in their lives, Ann and Bernie had begun to enjoy the comfort and relaxation that a successful business and completion of their child-raising tasks had brought them. At the age of forty-four, Ann unintentionally became pregnant. It had been more than twenty years since Ann and Bernie had cared for infant children. Some of their contemporaries were now becoming grandparents, and the thought of caring for a newborn child filled the couple with embarrassment and concern that the comfort they had worked so hard to achieve would now be spent starting over again with an infant. Because of these considerations, Ann and Bernie decided to have an abortion.[18]

Scenario 2

Donna and Jeremy, both in their mid-thirties, were a hardworking, economically comfortable couple. Jeremy was an accountant, and Donna, a restaurant manager. Donna and Jeremy had been trying to get pregnant for two years. After so many unsuccessful and disappointing months of trying, they decided to use in vitro fertilization (combining his sperm with her eggs), which is a common medical technique for infertile couples. To increase their odds of success, Donna and Jeremy's doctor suggested implanting four sets of zygotes each fertile cycle, a standard practice of infertility specialists. The in vitro fertilization worked, and Donna and Jeremy were finally a pregnant couple. However, soon after discovering they were pregnant, their doctor informed them that three of the four implants attached themselves to the uterus, meaning that not only were they pregnant, but they were to have triplets. Donna and Jeremy were not opposed to having three children, but they were financially prepared to accommodate only one child at this point. Since all three embryos appeared healthy, they randomly selected two for abortion and kept one to bring to term.

Scenario 3

Susan and Charles, both in perfect health, were in the fifth year of their marriage. Aside from his love for Susan, the prospect of raising a family was the most important thing in Charles's life—more important than career, possessions, sports, or any of the other things thought to be of utmost importance to men. Susan, on the other hand, was secretly ambivalent about having children, because she was indecisive about whether she wanted a career or a family. But because of her love for Charles and the fear of causing him what she believed might be unnecessary anxiety, she allowed him to believe that her reluctance was only with *when,* rather than with *whether,* to have children. And despite reasonable efforts at birth control, Susan became pregnant just at the point when her career took a significant turn for the better. At this moment, it was a career rather than children that she wanted, and she decided to have an abortion. Distraught, Charles tried to dissuade her by offering to forgo his own career and to take on the role traditionally reserved for mothers, but to no avail.[19]

Explain why you believe each abortion was justifiable or not and whether you believe it would be justifiable according to what you know of Jewish law. Your answer should include your own assumptions about the personhood of the fetus and your understanding of what constitutes physical and mental health.

For Your Group

Role-Playing

Divide into three small groups. Have each group prepare a three- to five-minute skit of one of the scenarios presented earlier in this unit. The groups should feel free to add or embellish any of the traits of the characters or to add more characters. After observing each skit, the whole group discusses the dilemma at hand, including the emotions involved and possible alternative ways that the characters could have dealt with their moral issue.

Research and Brainstorm

Divide into three small groups and assign each group one of the scenarios presented earlier in this unit. Allow fifteen to twenty minutes for the groups to research the moral issues and conclusions presented in the readings and in this unit. The goal is to understand what Rabbi Dorff might conclude about the scenario and why. Then each group presents its assigned scenario, being sure to cover the following points:

- Rabbi Dorff's possible conclusions regarding the scenario
- Why the group agrees or disagrees with the rabbi
- Other reasonable alternative solutions, if any, to the dilemma

Journal Work: Reflection

Answer the following question. Feel free to share your answer with a partner.

1. After having worked through this unit, has your stance on abortion changed or been refined in any way? Explain.

Summary

Americans, both Jews and non-Jews, find abortion to be a heated topic in political and ethical arenas. The influence of classic Christianity's views on abortion—and sex, for that matter—is one factor that has pushed us to think deeply about the moral issues embedded in this subject. Another factor that pushes us to think about the morality of abortion is simply that, as human beings, we have an innate psychological investment and connection to birth. Conception and birth evoke many powerful emotions, as we witness the miracle of a human life forming before our very eyes.

Some of the many issues that play a role in determining how we might think about the morality of abortion are determining when life begins, whether a fetus is a person, the status of the mother (physically, mentally, and economically, and her fiduciary relationship with the fetus), and the right of other parties to intercede (e.g., the father, the state). These issues touch on the very essence of what it is to be a human being and a parent, physically, psychologically, and spiritually. It is, therefore, important, especially considering the public nature of this moral issue, to understand the assumptions we are making about our humanity and our responsibilities as human beings.

Recommended Reading for Unit 5

Feldman, David M. *Birth Control in Jewish Law: Marital Relations, Contraception, and Abortion As Set Forth in Classic Texts and Jewish Law* (New York: Greenwood Publishing Group, 1980).

Unit 6 – Infertility

Readings

▪ *Matters of Life and Death:* Chapters 3 and 4

May it be Your will, O God . . . that You give me seed that is desirable, worthy, good, wholesome, proper, and accepted, which will be fit to exist and to mature without any sin or guilt. Bless me and my house with offspring, so that I shall know peace in my home, and may You endow my seed with vitality, spirit, and soul from the pure and holy source. . . . I beseech you, Lord of Hosts.

—Jacob ben Abraham, *Ma'aneh Lashon*

The prospect of having a child can be an experience filled will excitement and awe. Conversely, a couple that is unable to get pregnant can have an experience filled with agony and misery. Infertility, defined by Rabbi Dorff as when a couple is actively trying to have a child over the period of a year and cannot conceive or when the woman repeatedly miscarries, can be an excruciating source of frustration. Many couples feel embarrassed and inadequate when they discover that they are infertile. Infertility also brings a tremendous amount of tension to some marriages, sometimes even causing the marriage to fall apart. Sadly, one in seven couples in the United States is infertile due to various causes, such as ovulatory dysfunction (25 to 45 percent) and spermatozoal disorders (20 to 35 percent).[20] It is noteworthy to mention that 20 percent of the causes for infertility cannot be determined.

In Gen. 30:1, Rachel begs, "Give me children, or I shall die." The matriarch Sarah also suffered the pain of barrenness and gave her handmaid to her husband so that they might have a child. Hannah, in 1 Samuel, was so distraught over not having a child that she stopped eating; while weeping, she made a vow to God in the hope that she might have a child. Needless to say, Judaism recognizes the heartache and problems that infertility can bring. However, despite the fact that the commandment to procreate and the blessing of children are extremely important aspects of Judaism, a person's ability to procreate does not determine one's value and worth, nor does the tradition command a person to do something that he or she cannot fulfill.

Because Judaism is so aware of both the significance of having children and the problems of infertility, Jews have, since ancient times, tried many solutions and treatments for infertility. For example, the Hasidei Ashkenaz, believing that the psychological state of the woman can have an affect on fertility, tried early forms of psychotherapy. In the medieval period, many Jews dabbled with sorcery and magic ("practical kabbalah") and tried folk remedies for infertility that included prayers, incantations, magic symbols, amulets, and potions. Maimonides, the most influential medieval Jewish physician, tried medical solutions that addressed practical problems, such as increasing sexual desire, regulating body temperatures, and treating diseases of the generative parts.

Journal Work: Exploring Assumptions

Write short answers to the following questions. Feel free to share your answers with a partner.

1. What solutions or treatments do you know of for infertility?

2. Have you ever known an infertile couple? Did the couple try any treatments? If so, were any successful?

3. Do you believe that it is acceptable for a couple to use infertility treatments or should they be content with what life has dealt them? Would it be wrong for them *not* to try medical treatments?

Medical Technology

One of the most common techniques used for infertility is in vitro fertilization (IVF). This procedure involves fertilizing the ova outside of the body; to do this, the man's sperm and the woman's eggs are combined in a glass dish. Even though there are halakhic issues with IVF (e.g., selective abortions if multiple embryos are implanted in the uterus and the status of frozen embryos), rabbis generally permit it. There are, however, other solutions and techniques for fertility that are available in the United States, each of which has halakhic concerns.[21]

- *Surrogate mothers:* There are two types of surrogacy—ovum surrogacy uses the surrogate mother's eggs; gestational surrogacy uses the surrogate mother's womb as an incubator for the couple's eggs and sperm

- *Artificial insemination:* There are two types of artificial insemination—donated sperm is placed in the womb of the woman to fertilize her egg; or, donated eggs are combined with the sperm of the man (in a test tube) and then implanted in the uterus of the woman
- *Adoption:* Adopting a child who was born to and given up by another couple

Exercise

Read the sections in *Matters of Life and Death* pertaining to each of the infertility solutions and techniques and answer the following questions, adding your own views. Note that this extremely beneficial exercise is a bit time-consuming. Page numbers are provided to help you find the source text.

Surrogate Mothers

1. In ovum surrogacy, what problem may arise owing to the relationship between the surrogate mother and the child? (pp. 59–60)
2. Orthodox Rabbi Immanuel Jakobovits and Conservative Rabbi Daniel Gordis object to surrogacy because they believe it is degrading to the surrogate mother (e.g., using her for her reproductive abilities, underpaying her for her contribution, and limiting surrogacy to only the rich). Can you briefly summarize or outline the response to these objections given by Rabbi Dorff? (pp. 62–64)

Artificial Insemination Using Donated Sperm or Eggs

1. Some scholars have claimed that donor insemination is equivalent to adultery. What are Rabbi Dorff's arguments against this claim? (pp. 68–69)
2. In the case of sperm donation, some Orthodox rabbis prefer a non-Jewish donor for fear of unintentional incest, whereas others prefer a Jewish donor for fear of polluting the Jewish genetic line. What are Rabbi Dorff's responses to these preferences? (pp. 69–70)
3. In the case of sperm donation, the identity of the father raises four concerns: the child's Jewish identity, priestly status, and inheritance rights, and the father's fulfillment of the duty to procreate. The first three concerns are relatively simple to solve compared to the fourth. (pp. 72–73) How does the Conservative movement ultimately deal with the father's duty to procreate in the case of sperm donation? (p. 79)

41

4. In the case of donated eggs, how does the Conservative movement resolve the problem of determining who is the true mother? (p. 101)

Adoption

1. How do American and Jewish laws differ in the way they view adoptive parents? (p. 108)
2. Why is it difficult for Jews to adopt Jewish babies? May Jews adopt non-Jewish babies? (pp. 109–110)
3. What are some of the psychological issues that affect adoption? (pp. 110–111)

You Be the Rabbi

Read the following scenario from Genesis and then answer the questions that follow it.

Scenario

Sarai, Abram's wife, had borne him no children. She had an Egyptian maidservant whose name was Hagar. And Sarai said to Abram, "Look, the Lord has kept me from bearing. Consort with my maid; perhaps I shall have a son through her." And Abram heeded Sarai's request. So Sarai, Abram's wife, took her maid, Hagar the Egyptian—after Abram had dwelt in the land of Canaan ten years—and gave her to her husband Abram as a concubine. He cohabited with Hagar and she conceived (Gen. 16:1-4).

1. Do you believe that the infertility solution for Abram and Sarai was good or bad?
2. What other infertility solution or technique might be better, considering today's options, and why?

For Your Group

Create Your Own Dilemma

Divide into small groups. Give each group approximately ten minutes to devise and write down a thought-provoking and creative infertility dilemma that includes relevant details, such as age, economic status, familial tensions, and community pressures. The groups should include in their scenarios situations that could occur to the couple when learning of their infertility, when deciding about a solution, when trying a particular technique, and when looking back (even years later) at the solution they chose. Then have each group present its dilemma and solution to the whole group for further discussion.

If groups are having blocks in creativity, the facilitator can help by relating stories of infertility portrayed on television, in books, or in other media to help the members start generating their own ideas.

Some groups may prefer to role-play the dilemmas they created, which can be both useful and fun. Encourage the actors to display appropriate emotions.

Expressions in Prayer

Study the prayer from *Ma'aneh Lashon* at the beginning of this unit. Compare the emotional and poetic elements of that prayer with Hannah's prayer in Chapter 2 of 1 Sam. and the following nineteenth-century prayer:

> *I entreat you, Oh God, who graciously remembered our mothers Sarah and Hannah. Have mercy upon my lamentation, and remember me with the blessing of fruitlessness. Let our union be blessed with a strong and healthy child, in whom we may replant your holy religion. Hallow our life with your attention to this lofty matter. God, you know our pains; you know the painful empty heart of the childless. Have mercy and redeem us from this pain.*[22]

After comparing the prayers and discussing them, have group members write their own prayers for infertile couples in their journals. Be sure to discuss the role of compassion for infertile couples, both those who choose to use new techniques and those who do not. If individuals feel comfortable, they should share their prayers with the whole group.

Journal Work: Reflection

Write your answers to the following questions. Feel free to share your thoughts with a partner.

1. After studying this unit, has your stance on using infertility treatments changed or been refined? Explain.
2. If, God forbid, you or your spouse were faced with infertility, could you see yourself using an infertility treatment? If so, which would you prefer and why?

Summary

Popular attitudes in modern, Western civilization have shown much sympathetic concern for infertile couples. Communal compassion for infertile couples, both those who choose to try various techniques and those who do not, is immensely important. Technological and social advances have attempted to reduce infertility as much as possible, producing various avenues for couples in managing this misfortune. Thankfully, many couples have benefited from these solutions and techniques, which enable them to experience the joy and responsibility that a child brings.

Although divided on the support of some of these infertility solutions and techniques, the majority of Conservative Jews support them, on legitimate legal and philosophical grounds. Rabbi Dorff has been a major advocate in helping Jews understand the halakhic issues of infertility and discover a Jewish way to approach them. In the end, whatever solution an infertile couple chooses, they should be able to articulate their ethical assumptions and reasons for their choice and should be aware of its implications.

Recommended Reading for Unit 6

Gold, M. *And Hannah Wept* (Philadelphia: Jewish Publication Society, 1988).
Grazi, R. V. *Be Fruitful and Multiply* (Jerusalem: Feldheim, 1994).

Unit 7 – Parents and Children

Reading

- *Love Your Neighbor and Yourself:* Chapter 4; Appendix (optional)

Whetting Your Appetite

Nechama Leibowitz, a renowned Torah scholar and teacher, was famous for telling stories in which she learned things from unexpected sources. She told the following story of a time when she was grading papers in the back of a taxi:

*DRIVER: You are a teacher (*morah*), aren't you? Once upon a time, a teacher was called a "melamed." What is the difference between the two?*

NECHAMA: Nothing, they are the same.

DRIVER: No, there is a difference. I'll show you. Is whiskey good for you?

NECHAMA: No.

DRIVER: Do you drink whiskey?

NECHAMA: No.

DRIVER: If not, how do you know that it isn't good for you? I'll tell you how. If you sit in a bar and watch a respectable person when he begins to drink, and observe his behavior after several drinks, you understand that drinking whiskey is not good for you. That man becomes a melamed. *That is why the verse in Ps. 119:99 states, "from all my teachers (*melamdei – plural of* melamed*)" and not "from all my* morei."[23]

Exercise

Professor Leibowitz believed that this was a useful story to tell parents. What point or lesson do you think she might have wanted to convey through this story?

Family Life

With all of the hopes and dreams that prospective parents may have for their new children, the reality is that family life is not always so dreamy. The parent-child relationship, in particular, is one that is very complicated; along with its blessings can come hardships. In fact, rosy portrayals of these relationships on early television programs, such as *Ozzie and Harriet* and *Leave It to Beaver,* may have done more harm than good, since they presented an unrealistic representation of the average American family. Life is not clean and simple, and the parent-child relationship is influenced by all that life offers, the positive as well as the negative.

In the book *The Divine Secrets of the Ya-Ya Sisterhood,* which was made into a film in 2002, a more realistic depiction of a parent-child relationship (between a mother and daughter) is presented. The story shows how complications ensue as life, with all of its trials and tribulations, affects the sanctity of this relationship, sometimes producing long-lasting emotional and psychological wounds. However, given that so many of us have spent time in the therapist's office, we Americans do not need to read a book to know well that how a child is raised has a significant effect on what kind of adult he or she becomes.

We also know of the potential dreadful consequences of parent-child relationships because we have been witnesses to the most extreme examples of unhappy children and parents, hearing stories on the nightly news about people murdering their families and about children shooting children. Time and again, we wonder what it takes to be a good parent; what responsibilities do parents have to their children, and what responsibilities do children have to their parents?

Although Judaism does not assume that all families can or should be exactly the same, it has much to suggest about relationships between children and parents. The cornerstone of Jewish teachings and law in this regard is built on two verses from the Torah:

Honor your father and your mother, that you may long endure on the land that the Lord your God is assigning to you (Exod. 20:12; the fifth of the Ten Commandments).

You shall each revere his mother and his father, and keep My sabbaths: I the Lord am your God (Lev. 19:3).

These commands alone, however, may raise more questions than they answer, because they do not address what "honor" or "revere" means in practice or what obligations parents have to their children.

Journal Work: Exploring Assumptions

Write short answers to the following questions. Feel free to share your answers with a partner.

1. What are at least three obligations that parents have to their children? Which is the most important?
2. What are at least three obligations that children have to their parents?
3. In practical terms, what do you think it means to honor or revere your parents?
4. Why do you believe that parents and children have such obligations?
5. Is there ever a situation in which a child's obligations to his or her parents do not apply?

Parental Obligations

There is one primary text that explains a parent's obligations to a child:

Our Rabbis taught: A man is responsible to circumcise his son, to redeem him [from Temple service if he is the first born, pidyon ha-ben], *to teach him Torah, to marry him off to a woman, and to teach him a trade, and there are those who say that he must also teach him to swim. Rabbi Judah says: Anyone who fails to teach his son a trade teaches him to steal (B.* Kiddushin *29a).*

The classic Jewish sources do not say exactly why a parent has such duties, but it can be inferred that all the duties aim to initiate the child into the Jewish tradition (such as the covenant with God, a common community and historical identity, and shared moral values) and to preserve the Jewish people for another generation through a proper marriage and economic and physical survival. These are not necessarily easy obligations to fulfill, especially today when a Jewish education is so expensive.

In the section titled "Parental Duties: Applying Jewish Classical Sources to Contemporary Circumstances," Rabbi Dorff thoroughly examines each of these obligations.

Applying the Tradition

It should be noted that when we speak of children's obligations to their parents, we are referring to children beyond the age of bar or bat mitzvah (twelve or thirteen). Certainly, some of the obligations that children have for their parents may apply to the young, but according to Jewish law (*halakhah*), before a child reaches the age of bar or bat mitzvah he or she is not legally responsible for anything.

The obligations a child has for his or her parents appear to be attitudes (honor and reverence), but Judaism, because of its legal approach, generally translates those attitudes into specific behaviors.

Analyzing the Law

Review the two Torah verses printed earlier in this unit on p. 46, and then read the following passages from Jewish classical sources that interpret and reflect on those verses. Working alone or with a partner, analyze the source material and write or discuss answers to the questions that follow the passages.

Jewish Source Material

- "Our Rabbis taught: What is reverence and what is honor? Reverence means that he [the son] must neither stand in his [the father's] place, nor sit in his place, nor contradict his words, nor tip the scales against him [in an argument with others]. Honor means that he must give him food and drink, clothe and cover him, lead him out and take him in" (B. *Kiddushin* 31b).

- "'Lead him out'—How is this to be done? The son is obliged to accompany his father and mother, and not turn his back until they are out of sight. 'Take him in'—How is this to be done? He is obliged to give them a fitting dwelling, or rent one for them. And when the father or mother enters the son's home, he must rejoice in their coming and receive them happily" (*Menorat Ha-ma'or*).

- "There are three partners in the creation of every human being: the Holy One, blessed be He, the father, and the mother. The father provides the white matter, from which are formed the bones, sinews, nails, brain, and white part of the eye. The mother provides the red matter from which are formed the skin, flesh, hair, and pupil of the eye. The Holy One, blessed be He, infuses into each person breath, soul, features, vision, hearing, speech, power of motion, understanding, and intelligence" (B. *Niddah* 31a).

- "It is forbidden for a man to impose too heavy a yoke upon his children by being overly insistent on his due honor, for he thereby brings them close to sinning. Instead he should forgive and turn aside, for a father may forgo his honor if he wishes" (M.T. *Laws of Rebels* 6:8).

- "If one's father or mother becomes mentally disturbed, he should try to treat them as their mental state demands, until they are pitied by God. But if he finds that he cannot endure the situation because of their extreme madness, he may leave and go away, appointing others to care for them properly" (M.T. *Laws of Rebels* 6:10).

Questions

1. According to these sources, what does it mean, in practical terms, to honor and revere your parents?
2. What reason(s), if any, do these sources give for why it is important to fulfill these obligations to one's parents?
3. Are there limits to honoring parents and fulfilling one's obligations to his or her parents?

Further Thoughts

Aside from the attitudes of respect, honor, and reverence for parents (note that this list does not include love; Rashi claims that children are obligated to love their parents, but Maimonides claims that children are required only to honor, revere, and obey them), Rabbi Dorff notes that children's obligations to parents fit under the rubrics of "fulfilling parents' physical needs" and "personal presence." Rabbi Dorff also points out that the sources indicate that a parent should not make unreasonable demands on children. Furthermore, if a child cannot bear the burden of responsibility for a parent (e.g., due to a mental illness or the need of long-term medical treatment), a child can transfer some of that responsibility to others (e.g., housing for the elderly).

Review "Caring for Elderly Parents in Today's World" on pp. 139–143 in *Love Your Neighbor and Yourself*. Then read the following scenario and answer the question that follows it. You might want to work in small groups or with a partner.

Scenario

Emma's mother, Sophie, is in her late eighties and lives alone. Sophie has a hard time doing things on her own, as she suffers from very poor eyesight, poor hearing, and emphysema. Not only does she run out of breath going from the living room to her kitchen—because of the emphysema—but she loses her balance quite easily because of her lack of sensual perception (glasses and hearing aids do not seem to help). Thus, Sophie has fallen several times and has broken her ribs.

Despite her job as a teacher, Emma has been caring for her mother as best she can; but because Sophie's condition has been worsening each year, Emma is now not able to keep up with her other responsibilities while providing Sophie with adequate care. Emma has suggested to Sophie that it would be best if she went to a nursing home where there would be reliable, round-the-clock care. However, Sophie stubbornly refuses; she wants to stay at her own home because she is embarrassed by the fact that she cannot see or hear people and, ultimately, because she wants to die at home. Emma feels that her mother is not considering how difficult this makes her life, and this has caused a rift in their relationship.

Presently, Emma has hired a private in-home aide to care for Sophie every other day; the aide's duties include preparing meals, helping with household chores, and helping Sophie to shower and dress. The private aide is quite expensive, and Emma does not know how long she or Sophie will be able to afford it. In addition, even though Sophie knows that Emma works, she resents the fact that Emma is not taking care of these responsibilities herself.

Now assume that you have been hired by Emma and Sophie's family as an ethical consultant because neither Emma nor Sophie is happy with the current arrangements but wants to do the right thing. Considering what you have read regarding obligations between parents and children, how might you advise these two women and their family? What is the right thing for each of them to do in this case?

For Your Group

At the Movies

As a group, view a film about parents and children (some suggestions are listed below) as a group. Each member should watch with pencil and paper in hand and write down five questions pertaining to some of the moral issues that are raised between parents and children in the movie. After the movie is over, group members are encouraged to share their questions with the others as a basis for discussion. Make sure to apply the readings regarding children's obligations to parents and parents' obligations to children to the questions and to the discussion.

There are several films that convey many of the relevant moral issues that have been discussed in this unit. Here are a few recommendations (in order of my preference):

- *Parenthood* (1989; PG-13): a touching comedy that poignantly addresses many parent-child issues across several generations of children and parents
- *Life as a House* (2001; R): a story of a broken family that slowly reconstructs itself
- *American Beauty* (2000; R): an intense look at a seemingly ordinary suburban family, whose marriage and lives slowly unravel
- *Divine Secrets of the Ya-Ya Sisterhood* (2002, PG-13): a story about the evolving complications in relationships, especially between mothers and daughters

Journal Work: Reflection

Answer the following questions. Feel free to share your answers with a partner.

1. In light of what you have learned in this unit, what do you think it means to honor and revere your parents?
2. Why do you believe that parents and children have obligations to one another?

Summary

Nahum Sarna, in his commentary on the fifth commandment in Exodus—to honor your father and your mother—said, "Family life is the bedrock on which Jewish society stands."[24] Upholding the duties that we have to our parents and to our children surely is a principal element of that bedrock. In the Jewish tradition, honoring one's parents ultimately knows no bounds other than the two exceptions of a parent ordering a child to transgress the Torah (M. *Bava Metzi'a* 2:10) and a child ignoring parents' wishes when choosing a wife (*Yoreh De'ah* 250:25). In addition, children may use the aid of others to provide parental care if they cannot do that themselves.

However, as discussed, parents must ensure their children are brought up properly into the community and are given an education and a trade. Sadly, not all of our relationships with our parents or our children can be ideal, because the pains of life lead to personal and familial strain. Nonetheless, Judaism affirms that maintaining parent-child obligations offers a reward. Jews know that this reward is real, as we have witnessed it in the survival of generations of our people and the values that we uphold.

Recommended Reading for Unit 7

Blidstein, Gerald J. *Honor Thy Father and Mother: Filial Responsibility in Jewish Law* (New York: KTAV, 1975).

Diamant, Anita, with Karen Kushner. *How to Be a Jewish Parent: A Practical Handbook for Family Life* (New York: Schocken Books, 2000).

Unit 8 – Family Violence

Reading

- *Love Your Neighbor and Yourself:* Chapter 5

Most of us have heard the saying "Don't air your dirty laundry in public." This cautionary expression promotes secrecy to maintain an image of respectability. Until the 1960s, family violence—categorized as either sexual, verbal, or physical abuse against a spouse, child, parent, or elder—was considered such dirty laundry. However, since then there has been much social change, and although family violence in the United States is still all too often considered best kept as a secret, at least now it is publicly defined as behavior that needs to be brought into the light of public scrutiny so it can be curtailed.

Moreover, today we have laws that forbid family violence and that provide social services, such as shelters for battered women and for child abuse intervention. Also, the media has been helpful in promoting awareness of family violence and its terrible consequences. While modern moral theorists and sociologists disagree about the cause of family violence and what the public policy should be (keeping in mind that there are only a few decades of research), none of them argues that family violence is morally good, and each of them defines it as a topic of public concern.

One may think that Judaism would obviously be unanimous in its stance against abusing another individual, especially another family member. The classical sources of the tradition clearly state that no one has the right to strike another, and they specify penalties for such behavior. Surprisingly, however, there are sources that permit and even encourage some forms of family violence in the name of discipline—particularly wife beating (e.g., Rabbi Moses Isserles, the "Rema," condones a man beating his wife if she degrades him) and child beating. Consequently, the assumptions we have about the Jewish tradition, often colored by the movement we follow, influence our interpretations of such sources. Five reactions that Jews tend to have toward these classical Jewish sources are acceptance, denial, apologetics, rejection, and evasiveness.

Journal Work: Exploring Assumptions

Write short answers to the following questions. Feel free to share your answers with a partner.

1. Is there a justifiable reason for either beating or verbally assaulting a spouse, child, or parent? If so, what is the reason?

2. If you believe that there is never a justifiable reason for beating or verbally assaulting a spouse, child, or parent, on what grounds is your belief based?

3. How should a Jew use and interpret the sources that permit or encourage wife beating? Child beating?

4. Is there a difference between beating or verbally assaulting a family member and beating or verbally assaulting a stranger? If so, explain the difference(s) and/or provide an example to illustrate the difference(s).

Spousal Abuse

As Rabbi Dorff states in the reading for this unit, "The core methodological conviction of Conservative Judaism . . . is that we must understand sources within their historical context and make judgments about when and how to use them that are appropriate to our own time and our moral and theological convictions."[25] Thus the Conservative movement declared wife and husband beating prohibited by Jewish law. In addition, the Torah and Jewish tradition ban beating parents and sexual abuse. The tradition is keenly aware that family violence causes not only physical injury but also dishonor, embarrassment, and psychological damage.

Child Abuse

Of all the forms of abuse, beating a poorly behaved child is probably the most controversial. Many of us, particularly from older generations, are not unfamiliar with spankings, a slap on the hand, or even a paddle to the behind. There are also those of us who will never condone, under any circumstances, touching a child in any of these ways. This controversy is illuminated by the fact that the American Academy of Pediatrics took seven years to make a decision on spanking, concluding that it is "of limited effectiveness" and that it has "potentially deleterious side effects."[26] Within the Jewish tradition, one may find support for both sides.

Take a Stance

Read the following quotes from classical Jewish sources and think about what the Jewish stance should be on beating a child who behaves poorly. Try to identify the moral principle justifying the stance that you have recommended.

Jewish Source Material

- "If a man has a wayward and defiant son, who does not heed his father or mother and does not obey them even after they discipline him, his father and mother shall take hold of him and bring him out to the elders of his town at the public place of his community. . . . Thereupon the men of his town shall stone him to death. Thus you will sweep out evil from your midst: all Israel will hear and be afraid" (Deut. 21:18–21).

- "A wayward and defiant son [subject to execution in Deut. 21:18–21] never was and never will be" (B. *Sanhedrin* 71a).

- "Do not withhold discipline from a child; if you beat him with a rod he will not die. Beat him with a rod and you will save him from the grave" (Prov. 23:13–14).

- "Just as chopping of wood is an act of free choice [with full right to do so], even so are excluded [from the usual penalties for assault] the cases of a father who strikes his son, of a teacher that harasses his pupil, and of the agent of the court [who administers the punishment of an offender]" (M. *Makkot* 2:2).

- "If you must strike a child, strike him with the string of a shoe" (B. *Bava Batra* 21a).

- "He who does not rebuke his son leads him into delinquency" (*Shemot Rabbah* 1).

What do you think the Jewish tradition tells us about beating a child? Write your thoughts down or discuss them with a partner.

The Conservative Movement's Stance

In September 1995, the Conservative movement's Committee on Jewish Laws and Standards (CJLS) passed Rabbi Dorff's legal responsum by a vote of sixteen to one, decreeing:

> [We] Conservative rabbis would acquiesce to a light smack on the buttocks (a "potch") or even striking the child elsewhere on the body with an open hand (but not punch or pummeling with a fist). Only those types of contact that do not produce bleeding or a bruise would be permissible. . . . [We] forbid striking a child with a rod, belt, or instrument of any kind. We also hereby declare that, as we interpret and apply the Jewish tradition in our day, it clearly and emphatically prohibits a parent's use of corporeal punishment to the point of abuse—i.e., where the child is seriously harmed or where the punishment is clearly excessive as a response to the child's misdeed.[27]

It is important to note that Rabbi Dorff adds that parents should limit physical punishment "or, even, better, refrain from it altogether." There is sociological and psychological support for the idea that children imitate parents by doing to others what parents do to them.[28] Therefore, if we want to educate and discipline our children in a manner that leads to appropriate behavior (i.e., not growing up to strike others), it may be best to not use physical punishment at all.

Exercise

Answer the following questions to help you compare your stance with that of the Conservative movement.

1. List similarities and differences between your stance and that of the Conservative movement.
2. What assumptions about beating a child do you have in common with the Conservative movement? What assumptions are different?
3. Considering your own assumptions and what you know about Judaism, what reasonable arguments can you pose against the Conservative movement's stance?

For Your Group

The Interview

One person in the group is given the following scenario to read privately; no other person in the group is allowed to read it. While that person is reading, another member is designated as "interviewer."

Scenario

You were in the grocery yesterday, and as you were shopping you noticed a mother, her little boy, and her baby (who was sitting in the shopping cart). The little boy, about nine years old, was running around, taking items off of the shelves and dropping them, and pushing the cart with the baby in it away from the mother and laughing. He was simply behaving badly, making it difficult for the mother to shop and to be attentive to the infant. After witnessing this boy carrying on a couple of times, you found yourself on the beverage aisle. As you put a bottle of soda in your cart, you turned and saw the boy accidentally ram the cart into the shelving, knocking down several cans of soft drink. The mother then yelled at the boy, saying, "I told you to stop!" She then grabbed him and slapped him in the face hard enough so that you could hear the slap. The boy, stunned and hurt, rubbed his face and cried loudly.

After the designated person takes a moment to read the scenario, he or she rejoins the rest of the group and sits next to the interviewer. Everyone else acts as witnesses, sitting so that they can observe the interview. The interviewer asks the questions listed below (adding, subtracting, or amending questions as he or she sees fit). However, given that individuals will be performing in front of others (at times improvising), before conducting the interview everyone should be reminded that a group functions best in a warm and accepting atmosphere and that everyone should be given the utmost respect for their participation.

Interview Questions

1. Can you describe, in your own words, what you witnessed? Be as detailed as possible, but do not read the scenario to us.
2. How did you feel when you witnessed the boy misbehaving before he was slapped?
3. Did you think that there was anything that the mother could have done to prevent the boy from misbehaving before it escalated to the slap?

4. How did you feel when you saw the boy being slapped?

5. Did you think that a slap was justified in this circumstance? Why?

6. Why do you believe the mother slapped the boy—what purpose(s) did she think it would serve?

7. Is there something else that the mother could have done, other than slap her son, to accomplish that same goal?

8. If you were the mother, what would you have done differently? The same?

After the interview is completed, and the two performers are given praise for their efforts, the discussion is opened up to the rest of the group. Topics that could be included in the discussion are as follows:

- What do you think about what the mother did?
- Do you agree with the one who was interviewed?
- Is it ever okay to hit a child? Why?
- What should we do if we are ever witnesses to someone hitting a child inappropriately?

The readings for this unit contain Rabbi Dorff's in-depth analysis of these issues.

Journal Work: Reflection

Answer the following question. Feel free to share your answer with a partner.

1. After working through this unit, has your stance on spanking children in the name of discipline changed or been refined in any way? Explain.

Summary

Family violence is a legitimate personal, familial, and social concern that can be found across all areas of the societal spectrum and in all cultures, religions, and socioeconomic classes. The issues surrounding family violence that need to be addressed are identifying abuse (physical, sexual, or verbal), deciding what to do once it has been identified, recognizing the consequences of it, and learning how to prevent it from recurring. Undoubtedly, this is all very complicated, especially considering that the abuse sometimes happens within our own families and among the people we love and to whom we are closest.

Jewish views of family violence and the issues that surround it are deeply rooted in Jewish views of God and humanity. The primary concept and belief that informs the Jewish point of view is that we all have the divine image of God within us; thus, we need to be treated with respect. That divine image should never be sacrificed because of frustration or anger we may feel toward another. No one ever deserves to be humiliated in such a way so that his or her divine image is compromised. Family violence jeopardizes this basic Jewish belief possibly more than any other act, and it may be the most painful and humiliating experience that one can have. Furthermore, family violence produces some of the worst potential consequences for a human being in terms of emotional and spiritual well-being. Judaism calls for humanitarian and decent behavior, because we all depend on it—not only in our families but in the whole world.

Recommended Reading for Unit 8

Graetz, Naomi. *Silence Is Deadly: Judaism Confronts Wifebeating* (Northvale, NJ: Aronson, 1998).

Russ, Ian, Sally Weber, and Ellen Ledley, eds. *Shalom Bayit: A Jewish Response to Child Abuse and Domestic Violence* (Los Angeles: Jewish Family Service and the University of Judaism, 1993).

Unit 9 – Poverty

Reading

- *To Do the Right and the Good:* Chapter 6

Whetting Your Appetite

God stands together with the poor person at the door, and one should therefore consider Whom one is confronting. (Lev. Rabbah 34:9)

Exercise

Answer the following questions.

1. Read the opening quote for this unit. What do you think the rabbis intended to teach us?

2. Is this quote particularly meaningful for you? Why or why not?

Economic Diversity

One of the strangest aspects of living in a large city in the United States is how quickly we can go from a very wealthy neighborhood to a very poor neighborhood. In Los Angeles, for example, we can drive along Rodeo or Beverly drives, famous for their affluence, but after continuing just a few miles, we drive along Venice or Crenshaw boulevards, through a much lower-income area. As we travel through such a city, the apparent economic status of the neighborhoods changes so drastically and quickly that it is easy to wonder if they are even part of the same city at all. This sort of transition may become familiar to city dwellers, but it is always noticeable.

The division of the economic classes has existed in societies for thousands of years. Just as today one can be approached by a beggar in a subway station or outside of a convenience store, one could just as easily have been approached by a beggar in the city streets of medieval Paris or ancient

Athens. All sorts of civilized societies have experienced this issue, and there have been a variety of economic policies and philosophies employed to respond to the poor. Under feudalism, for example, there was a sharp and distinct separation of the classes. Libertarian philosophies claim that individuals get what they deserve or earn what they have. Some societies have adopted socialism, which tries to achieve the ideal of social and economic equality, although some socialist societies offer more variation in individual initiative for wealth than others. Communism (as in today's China) asserts that everyone equally owns all goods that are produced. The United States, of course, is a capitalist society that recompenses individuals for skills and efforts, as well as provides some security for those who have not been able to succeed in the free-market competition.

Jews throughout history have lived under many different governments and have experienced many different economic and political conditions. This has influenced the Jewish community's views and has given rise to several changes of perspective as to how Jews understand what our obligations to the poor might be. Nevertheless, as Rabbi Dorff points out, "Jewish ideology, ethics, and law . . . affirm that it is an obligation of both the individual and the community to care for the poor and ultimately to bring them out of poverty. . . . [R]esponsibility to the poor has endured as an essential ingredient both in Jewish values and in Jewish practice."[29]

Journal Work: Exploring Assumptions

Write short answers to the following questions. Feel free to share your answers with a partner.

1. Do you think that the wealthy have any obligation to aid the poor financially? Why or why not?
2. Why do you believe that someone should *not* give to the poor? List as many reasons as possible.
3. Why do you believe that someone *should* give to the poor? List as many reasons as possible.

Should We Give to the Poor?

Regardless of whether a person is politically conservative, moderate, liberal, or anything else, he or she asks the same types of questions when approached by a beggar: "Should I give this person money? What will he or she do with it? If I give money, how much should I give?" In the reading for this unit, Rabbi Dorff discusses the basic reasons people usually mention for not giving money to the poor as well as the Jewish theological tenets that undergird Jewish laws concerning the poor. Table 2 provides a summary.

Table 2. Giving to the Poor: Pro and Con

Common Reasons for Not Giving to the Poor	Jewish Tenets Concerning the Poor
The poor do not work for a living and, therefore, do not deserve our help	*Pikuach nefesh:* saving or guarding a human life
Offering help to the poor may be detrimental to them because they may come to depend on it	*Community:* caring for the poor exemplifies and expresses our existence and character as a community
Sometimes giving money to the poor actually contributes to their harmful habits	*Compassion:* part of the Jewish historical and spiritual identity is to be sensitive to the indignity and slavery that poverty produces
You never know whether people who beg for money actually need it or whether they are deceiving you	*God's commandment:* in the Torah, God commands us to care for the poor
Beggars might pose a danger to you, because if they don't get what they want they may attack you	*Acknowledgment of God's dominion over the earth and humanity:* God is owner of all property, and so not giving to the poor denies God's sovereignty
Beggars are bothersome; people should be able to walk the streets without being accosted for money	*The dignity of being God's creature:* being human means that we have a higher status than all other creatures; and caring for the poor, as their status deserves, is our privilege and duty
The guilt we feel with each beggar who panders for money makes it difficult to choose whom to give to and when	*Membership in God's covenanted community:* honoring the dignity of the poor fulfills both the letter of the law and the spirit of the covenant
Begging is demeaning, and we do not want to encourage demeaning behavior in society	*Aspirations for holiness:* we are to care for the poor so we can be holy like God

Exercise

Answer the following questions.

1. Do the two sides of the argument concerning giving to the poor conflict with or contradict one another?

2. Do you think that any of the reasons or tenets presented in Table 2 are unreasonable? If so, which ones and why?

3. In terms of personal and communal significance, does one side of the issue seem to outweigh the other? Explain.

For Your Group

Values Ranking

Individually or in small groups, analyze the statements listed in Table 2. Rank the comments made in each column in order of importance and substance (1 = most important; 8 = least important). *Note:* There are no right or wrong rankings or methods of ranking. When you are finished, explain your reasons for picking the statements you rated 1 and 8 in each column. If you are working in a group, compare your rankings with the others and share your explanations.

Looking Deeper into the Tradition

Beginning with legal policies set forth in the Bible, the Jewish tradition offers many provisions and curative measures for the poor. Rabbinic law established forms of assistance, such as soup kitchens, medical attention, and—the most substantial aid—a charity fund. The Rabbis also created a hierarchical, need-based system to determine how to delegate resources to the needy. However, the Rabbis also seemed to realize that the best type of aid is preventing poverty in the first place, and they laid down several preventive measures, including educating children in a skill or trade that leads to pay, dowries for women so that they need not become beggars, imposing a one-sixth profit price on the sale of merchandise and food, making loans easy and accessible for all, and emphasizing employment opportunities for all. Because Jews were subjugated throughout history, they were often left without jobs and few employment opportunities. Therefore, it is not surprising to see what the highest form of charity is on Maimonides' famous list:

> *The highest merit in giving charity is attained by the person who comes to the aid of another in bad circumstances before he reaches the stage of actual poverty. Such aid may be in the form of a substantial gift presented in an honorable manner, or a loan, or the forming of a partnership with him for the transaction of some business enterprise, or assistance in obtaining some employment for him, so that he will not be forced to seek charity from his fellow men. Concerning this, Scripture [Lev. 25:35] says, "You shall strengthen him;" that is, you shall assist him so that he does not fall (M.T. Laws of Gifts to the Poor 10:7–14).[30]*

Jewish law though, as Maimonides alludes to, does not view the poor as mere appendages to the community who simply act as parasites; the poor, ultimately, have their own responsibilities.

Evaluating Jewish Writings

Individually or with a partner, read the quotes from classical Jewish sources concerning work and providing for others.

Jewish Source Material

- "The Lord God took the man and placed him in the garden of Eden, to till it and tend it" (Gen. 2:15).

- "A person should not say, 'I will eat and drink and see prosperity without troubling myself since Heaven will have compassion upon me.' To teach this, Scripture [Job 1:10] says, 'You have the work of his hands,' demonstrating that a man should toil with both his hands, and then the Holy One, blessed be God, will grant divine blessing" (*Tanhuma Va-yetse'* 13).[31]

- "Hadrian said to him, 'Old man, if you had worked earlier, there would be no need for you to work so late in life.' He replied, 'I have toiled both early and late, and what was pleasing to the Master of Heaven God has done with me.' Hadrian asked him how old he was, and the answer was 100. He then exclaimed, 'You are 100 years old, and you stand there breaking up the soil to plant trees! Do you expect to eat of their fruit?' He replied, 'If I am worthy, I will eat; but if not [and I die], as my fathers labored for me, so I labor for my children' " (*Lev. Rabbah* 25:5).

- "Even a poor person who lives entirely on charity must also give charity to another poor person" (B. *Bava Kamma* 119a).

Questions

If you are in a group, share and discuss your responses to these questions.

1. According to these sources, what are the implied reasons that people should work?
2. Considering that these quotations apply to the poor and rich alike, what can one assume is the ultimate goal of providing assistance to the needy?

Possible Answers

The Jewish tradition emphasizes that work and responsibility are part of the normative state of human existence and that they apply to everyone, including the poor. As Maimonides states, the highest form of charity, and the ultimate goal of charity altogether, is to help the poor become self-sustaining so that they can work and take on the responsibility of "working and tending the Garden."

Applying the Tradition

Certainly today, poverty is considered to be an ongoing problem. The challenges and potential consequences we face with poverty are very sad and, quite frankly, frightening. On this matter, Rabbi Dorff states:

> *From 1975 to 1994, the largest increase in poverty for children under six was not in urban or rural areas, but in suburbia. Today, "poor" is defined as a single person with an annual income of less than $7,740 or a family of four earning less that $15,600. Since the 1960s many of these people received benefits—such as housing subsidies, food stamps, Aid to Families with Dependent Children, and direct cash payments—that enabled them to achieve a minimal standard of living; but in the 1996 Welfare Reform Act, Congress put many of these programs in jeopardy. . . .*

> *As a result of rising costs and lower-paying jobs, an increasing number of families are at, or perilously near, the poverty line* even though at least one member of the family is employed.[32]

For Your Group

Divide into small "committees" of three or four people. Each committee reads the scenario presented below and is given approximately twenty-five minutes to brainstorm a solution for New York City. Each committee's solution should account for the following considerations:

- What the appropriate Jewish response would be—include whatever citations of Jewish sources you have available to support your plan
- The potential role of the federal government in enacting your plan

- The potential role of the Jewish community and its established services—such as Jewish Family Services, Jewish soup kitchens (e.g., Mazon and Sova), the local Jewish federation, and the local Jewish community centers
- The potential involvement and ramifications for New York citizens
- Legal responsibilities

Once each committee has completed its plan to resolve this problem, role-play a city council board meeting during which each group is given three to five minutes to propose its plan. (Each committee may want to designate someone to be its official representative and to voice its plan.) The other members of the group act as the city council. Make sure to allow time for questions and answers after each proposal. Suggested questions follow the scenario.

Scenario

Several years ago, New York City was the site of a major moral debate. At the urging of then Mayor Koch, the city council passed an ordinance that banned begging in the subways. Both the mayor and the city council expressed concern about the poor and the homeless, and indeed they tried to find increased city, state, and federal funds to alleviate the plight of the homeless in various ways. The city officials claimed, however, that public begging significantly diminishes the quality of life for all New Yorkers, and that people have a right to ride the subways without being accosted by beggars. They also were concerned that people would simply avoid public transportation if it included this kind of embarrassment and unpleasantness each time they rode. And if people did not use public transportation, traffic congestion, which was already unbearable, would increase. The federal court, however, declared the ordinance unconstitutional on the grounds that it interfered with the beggars' right to free speech guaranteed by the First Amendment of the Constitution.

Questions

If you are working individually, answer the following questions on your own. These questions can also be used to guide a group discussion.

1. From what you have read and what you have studied in this unit, what do you think is the proper Jewish response to the proposed New York City ordinance and the federal court's response to it? Cite whatever Jewish sources you have available to support your position.

66

2. How might others differently interpret the sources you chose to support your explanation? What alternative conclusion could be reached?

Journal Work: Reflection

Answer the following question. Feel free to share your answer with a partner.

1. After working through this unit, has your stance on caring for the poor on a personal or societal level changed or been refined? Explain.

Summary

Judaism acknowledges that poverty is and always will be an ongoing problem. As Deuteronomy 15:11 states, "For there will never cease to be needy ones in your land." There is also, however, another important and relevant teaching from the Rabbis: "You are not obliged to finish the task, but neither are you free to neglect it." (M. *Avot* 2:21) In regard to poverty, Jews have historically shown their acceptance of these teachings in their behavior, both taking note of the needy and continuously undertaking the task of doing whatever they could to provide for the needy. Jewish leaders throughout the ages have charged their communities to do whatever they could to care for the poor. As a community, Jews have, therefore, done a commendable job in responding to the poor, but there is clearly room for more work to be done.

Instead of the English word for "charity," Jews often use the Hebrew word "*tzedakah*," which is derived from the word "*tzedek*," literally meaning "justice." Thus a person who carries out *tzedakah,* in all of its forms, is called a "*tzadik*," a "righteous person." Rabbi Dorff speaks of the motivation for such righteous and just behavior:

We care for the poor because it is the just and righteous thing to do. We seek to be just and righteous ultimately because that is the holy and God-like choice.[33]

[B]ut perhaps the fundamental, underlying principle [of the Jewish conviction to care for the poor] is the dignity of the human being created in the image of God.[34]

67

Recommended Reading for Unit 9

Rubin, Gary, ed. *The Poor among Us: Jewish Tradition and Social Policy* (New York: American Jewish
    Committee, 1986).

Siegel, Danny. *Gym Shoes and Irises: Personalized Tzedakah* (Spring Valley, NY: Town House Press, 1982).

Additional Resources [35]

Better Homes Fund
181 Wells Avenue
Newton Centre, MA 02459
Voice: 617-964-3834
Fax: 617-244-1758

Studies the lives of homeless and low-income women and gives grants to organizations dealing with
homeless and welfare issues.

Food Research and Action Center
1875 Connecticut Avenue N.W. Suite 540
Washington, D.C. 20009
Voice: 202-986-2200
Fax: 202-986-2525
E-mail: Webmaster@frac.org
Web: www.frac.org

Works with state policymakers to urge them to choose options of the new welfare law that keep in
place supports for food and nutrition. Also helps advocates for legal immigrants to learn about
exemptions from exclusion.

Mazon: A Jewish Response to Hunger
12401 Wilshire Boulevard
Los Angeles, CA 90025
Voice: 310-442-0020
Fax: 310-442-0030
E-mail: mazonmail@aol.com
Web: www.shamash.org/soc-action/mazon

Raises funds from the Jewish community nationally (especially through the gifts of a percentage of
the cost of a bar or bat mitzvah or a wedding) to support Jewish and non-Jewish organizations that
provide food for the hungry.

Unit 10 – War

Reading

- *To Do the Right and the Good:* Chapter 7

I can't believe the news today, I can't close my eyes and make it go away.

How long, how long must we sing this song? How long? . . .

Broken bottles under children's feet, bodies strewn across a dead end street. . . .

And the battle's just begun, there's many lost, but tell me who has won?

The trenches dug within our hearts, and mothers, children, brothers, sisters torn apart.

How long, how long must we sing this song? How long?

—U2, "Sunday Bloody Sunday"

Many of us in the United States have neither been in a war nor suffered as direct victims of war, but on September 11, 2001, between 8:45 and 9:40 in the morning, when the Pentagon and the twin towers of the World Trade Center were bombed by fuel-filled airplanes seating almost two hundred passengers, we sure felt like we were in a war. As we watched the news like addicts who could not get enough, we often found ourselves without much to say other than emotional outbursts. Across the airwaves, the lyrics to the famous song above by the Irish band U2 might as well have been playing every hour, as they undoubtedly express what most of us felt at some point and continue to feel about that horrendous calamity. This tragedy and the cry of the vocalist—"How long?"—have come to remind us of what has happened in the past and what will inevitably be in the future, awakening us again to Jomini's words in *The Art of War:* "The greatest tragedy is war, but so long as there is mankind, there will be war."[36]

In the past several decades, with Israel showing itself to be a significant military power and with the images of strong Israeli soldiers on television and in the newspapers, it is easy to forget that, historically, Jews have had political and military autonomy for only three relatively brief periods: Moses to the destruction of the First Temple (1300–586 B.C.E.), the Maccabean period (168–63

B.C.E.), and the modern State of Israel (1948–present). Therefore, most of the decisions about wars—that Jews waged or observed—were made by the governments that ruled over them. However, with the military experiences and precedents set forth in the Bible by leaders such as Moses, Joshua, and David, as well as the account of the Maccabees, the Jewish tradition has produced guidance and legal decisions in regard to the issues that surround war.

Journal Work: Exploring Assumptions

Write short answers to the following questions. Feel free to share your answers with a partner.

1. What was your immediate response to the September 11 terrorist attacks? If you prefer, write about another warlike experience that may have touched you (e.g., Vietnam, the Gulf War, or the *intifada* in Israel).
2. What do you believe is a just response to what happed on September 11? Why?
3. What is your concept of a "just war"? Is any war just?

Biblical Notions

In biblical times, nations believed that their gods were the leaders of their armies. Israel also believed this, referring to God as "the Warrior" (Exod. 15:3) and carrying the ark onto the battlefield to symbolize divine presence (Num. 10:35). Because God is unconquerable, they attributed it to a lack of their own faith in God when there was a military defeat. Most of the biblical laws for wars are given in Deuteronomy 20.

Studying with the Rabbis

Individually or with a partner, read Deuteronomy 20. It may be helpful to note the exemptions from military service mentioned in this chapter. Next, read the following rabbinic source material and answer the questions that follow.

Source 1

This first source begins by asking about the military exemptions mentioned in Deuteronomy.

To what do these [exemptions] apply? To discretionary wars (milhamot reshut), *but in wars commanded by the Torah* (milhamot mitzvah) *all go forth, even a bridegroom from his chamber and a bride from her canopy.[37] Rabbi Judah says: To what do these [exemptions] apply? To wars commanded by the Torah* (milhamot mitzvah), *but in obligatory wars* (milhamot hovah) *all go forth, even a bridegroom from his chamber and a bride from her canopy* (M. Sotah 8:7).

1. In this mishnah, Rabbi Judah counters the Sages' understanding of which wars apply to which exemptions in Deuteronomy. To what types of wars do the Sages give exemptions and to what types of wars does Rabbi Judah give exemptions? To what types of wars do the Sages *not* give exemptions and to which does Rabbi Judah *not* give exemptions?

2. Is Rabbi Judah arguing with the Sages or just adding to their statement? Explain.

Source 2

The Rabbis of the Talmud interpret what wars the Sages and Rabbi Judah are talking about:

Rabbi Yochanan said: "What the Sages call discretionary (*reshut*), is what Rabbi Judah calls commanded by Torah (*mitzvah*). And what the Sages call commanded by the Torah (*mitzvah*), is what Rabbi Judah calls obligatory (*hovah*)."

Rava said: "All [the Sages and Rabbi Judah] agree that the wars Joshua fought to conquer [the land of Israel] were all obligatory (hovah), *and all agree that the wars the House of David fought for the sake of gain were discretionary* (reshut). *So, when do they disagree? With regard to preemptive wars against those who seek to attack Israel.[38] [Regarding this type of war] Rabbi Judah calls it commanded by the Torah* (mitzvah). *Whereas [the Sages] call it discretionary* (reshut). *[Therefore] the practical difference between them is [whether one is fighting in such a war is regarded as] exempt from going, when he is engaged in performing another commandment of the Torah* (mitzvah) (B. Sotah 44b).

1. How does Rabbi Yochanan understand the differences in terminology given by the Sages and Rabbi Judah in the mishnah?

2. Would Rabbi Yochanan see any practical differences between the Sages and Rabbi Judah in regard to exemptions from war?

3. According to Rava, about what do the Sages and Rabbi Judah agree?

4. What does Rava think that the Sages and Rabbi Judah were arguing about?

5. According to Rava, if you were engaged in a mitzvah and a preemptive war was called, who would exempt you from that mitzvah for the sake of the war, the Sages or Rabbi Judah? Explain.

Understanding the Rabbis

Rabbi Dorff understands these rabbinic sources as teaching that there are three types of wars:

> [S]pecifically commanded wars, including the wars against the seven Canaanite nations and the war against Amalek; discretionary wars, including the wars of King David to expand the borders of the Israelite territory; and, for Rabbi Judah, indirectly commanded wars, including preemptive wars for the purposes of "diminishing the heathen so that they will not march against them [the Israelites]."[39]

Accordingly, Rabbi Judah would exempt someone from another mitzvah if he or she were engaged in an indirectly commanded war since it still constitutes a command, but the Sages would not.

Applying the Tradition

Although interpreted in varying ways by both medieval and modern rabbis, there is sufficient evidence in the Jewish tradition for other acceptable types of war, which Rabbi Dorff discusses in the reading for this unit: Namely, defensive wars, which were deemed important enough for the Rabbis to exempt individuals from keeping the Sabbath; preemptive wars for defense, which are the most controversial and bring on a wide spectrum of interpretations regarding their usage; wars for the sake of redeeming captives, which are understood to be extensions of the command to save and preserve life; and wars against non-Jews who fail to abide by the seven Noahide Laws, although there is more support in the tradition against engaging in such a war than there is condoning it.

It is important, however, that Rabbi Dorff notes four factors deterring Jews from wishing to engage in wars, even when the wars would be legitimate according to Jewish law:

- Waging war is not an honorable or glorified ideal as it is in some other cultures because, historically, Jews have often been the victims of war

- Respecting one's government, both the good and the bad, is a strong feature of the Jewish tradition, which may prevent Jews from considering military interventions to revolt against a government or to change its policies
- Judaism clearly understands the dehumanizing effects of wars, and there is a good deal of material in the tradition that speaks of preserving as much moral sensitivity as possible in a war
- Judaism strongly emphasizes the importance of peace

You Be the Judge

Read the scenario and answer the question about the Jewish tradition and ethics that follows.

The Story of the Lamed-Hey [Thirty-Five]

On January 15, 1948, during the months before the Declaration of Independence of the State of Israel but after the United Nations had approved the Partition Plan, hostilities had already begun between Arabs and Jews, with the British officially neutral but, in fact, giving support to the Arabs. The Jewish villages in the Ezion Block (Gush Ezion) lay southwest of Jerusalem, in the area that the United Nations had designated as Arab, but the Jews were intent on saving them as Jewish territory. The Jewish settlements were completely surrounded by hostile Arab villages, and they were in great need of reinforcements and supplies. A contingent of thirty-eight young men, all Hebrew University students, left Jerusalem at night in the hope of reaching the Jewish villages there. On the way, one broke his leg, and two returned the injured man to Jerusalem, leaving thirty-five to press on to Gush Ezion. At dawn, they came across an old Arab shepherd. They asked him for directions and then were faced with the question of what to do with him. If they killed him, they would be killing a noncombatant. Taking him prisoner would slow them down tremendously, adding to the danger of being discovered by Arabs. They did not have a rope to tie him up. They ultimately let him be and pushed on. As soon as they left, he ran to the nearest Arab village and alerted them of the Jewish brigade; ultimately, all thirty-five men were killed.[40]

Given what you have learned in this unit and from the reading and using 20/20 hindsight, what should the thirty-five men have done? Explain your answer using support from the Jewish tradition and ethical reasoning. If you are working with a group, share and discuss the various answers.

73

Furthering the Discussion

The attacks waged on the United States on September 11, 2001, and the story of the thirty-five men raise the topic of the killing of innocent people in the name of war or during a war. This presents a new angle from which to view the moral implications of war, especially considering that terrorism and killing large numbers of the innocent are now becoming a defining feature of war. On this topic, philosophy professor Richard Wasserstrom wrote:

> *If wars were conducted, or were likely to be conducted, so as to produce only the occasional intentional killing of the innocent, that would be one thing. We could then say with some confidence that on this ground at least wars can hardly be condemned as out of hand. Unfortunately, mankind no longer lives in such a world. . . .The intentional, or at least knowing, killing of the innocent on a large scale became a practically necessary feature of war with the advent of air warfare. And the genuinely indiscriminate killing of the very great numbers of innocent persons is the dominant legacy of the birth of thermonuclear weapons.*[41]

Exercise

Answer the following questions, or use the questions to launch and guide a group discussion.

1. Under what circumstances, if any, do you think terrorism is justified?

2. From what you have read and what you have studied in this unit, do you think the Jewish tradition would justify terrorism? Explain.

3. It could be argued that each person in a society contributes to the establishment and/or maintenance of that society by, for instance, their financial, electoral, or tacit support. In light of this argument, do you believe that anyone can really be considered "innocent" and free from being a target of war, because they are an integral part of the targeted regime? Explain.

Journal Work: Reflection

Answer the following question. Feel free to share your answer with a partner.

1. After working through this unit, has your concept of a "just war" changed or been refined in any way? Explain.

Summary

Although Judaism places a strong emphasis on the ideal of peace, there is a clear recognition in the tradition that war is a part of the human experience. Therefore, Judaism cannot truly be labeled as pacifistic, ultimately teaching that there is indeed "a time for war." However, even within the seemingly immoral context of war, there are moral sensitivities that need to be taken into account when waging war. The Bible and the Talmud offer us moral guidance in this regard; but, in fact, Judaism is not all that familiar with the political and military power associated with waging war, and thus the guidance that its sources offer is somewhat limited. Nevertheless, given the military technological advances in modern-day warfare and the frequency of terrorist acts in the name of war, the moral questions regarding war have become even more complex and in constant need of reexamination by all.

May we see the day when war and bloodshed cease,

when a great peace will embrace the whole world.[42]

Recommended Reading for Unit 10

Baron, Salo, and George S. Wise, eds. *Violence and Defense in the Jewish Experience.* (Philadelphia: Jewish Publication Society, 1977).

Shavit Artson, Bradley. *Love Peace and Pursue Peace: A Jewish Response to War and Nuclear Annihilation* (New York: United Synagogue Book Service, 1988).

Unit 11 – Dying: Suicide and Euthanasia

Readings

- *Matters of Life and Death:* Chapters 7 and 8

Whetting Your Appetite

Two fourteen-year-old boys on a hiking trip find themselves sitting near the edge of a cliff overlooking a lake. While contemplating the height of the cliff, the conversation quickly becomes very morbid:

"So would you rather die by falling off a cliff or drowning?"

"Falling off a cliff. Seven seconds and its over."

"How about getting eaten by a great white shark? That would be quick."

"Yeah, but that would be scary. Falling off a cliff might actually be fun for a moment."

"The worst would be getting buried alive. You'd be suffocating and no one could find you. I think I'd rather kill myself."

"For me, getting burned alive would be the worst 'cause it seems so painful."

Exercise

Answer the following questions.

1. Why do you think these teens would be talking about their deaths?
2. Why do you think they have preferences as to how they might die?

Thinking about Death

Despite the fact that gruesomeness and morbidity are common subjects and points of interest for young teens (evidenced by the movies and video games marketed toward them), for a lot of people, death is a sensitive and difficult topic. Nonetheless, regardless of how frightening the mystery of it might be, there is a time in everyone's life when we clearly realize that we are all going to die. Most of us, however, are able to continue living life without the fear of death crippling our behavior and preoccupying our thoughts; we are relatively content with the fact that we die, continuing to maintain hope, find meaning, and experience joy in what this life offers us. Therefore, most of us do not have a significant problem with accepting the inevitability of death, but as the dialogue above shows, how we die is a matter of more concern.

In ideal circumstances, each us would have made preparations for death and would have some role in deciding how we are to die. Before we die, many of us want to be able to put our material and familial affairs in order. Many of us would prefer to die with as little suffering as possible, with integrity, and surrounded by loved ones. Sadly, however, not everyone dies in such ideal circumstances, and often these preparations and preferences do not come to pass. For some, death, or the onset of death, comes quickly and unexpectedly, creating a difficult, complex, and painful situation for themselves and their family. For others, chronic, debilitating illnesses make one suffer and lose dignity for a long time before death finally comes.

As discussed in Unit 3, Judaism understands that our life is sacred because we are created in the image of God and that we should do all that we can to preserve life (*pikuach nefesh*), that we have responsibilities to our bodies because they belong to God, and that our bodies are put under our care with the potential of acting holy. In Deuteronomy 30:19, the Torah commands us to "choose life," implying that whatever life we have been given is special and worth living to its natural end. These moral assumptions certainly have repercussions for end-of-life issues, particularly pertaining to decisions of how to care for someone who is terminally ill.

Defining Terms

- *Murder:* The malicious taking of another's life without a legal excuse (such as self-defense or war)
- *Suicide:* The murder of oneself
- *Euthanasia:* From the Greek for "good" (*eu*) and "death" (*thanatos*); the act or practice of bringing about the death of a suffering individual, especially painlessly, for reasons considered merciful

- *Active euthanasia:* Euthanasia by actively taking a life—*voluntary* means the patient decides to end his or her life and actively implements this decision (suicide); *involuntary* means someone else takes deliberate action to accelerate the patient's death, but with the patient's consent and for the patient's welfare

- *Passive euthanasia:* Euthanasia by removing means that are prolonging the patient's life or by refusing to intervene in the process of the patient's natural demise—*voluntary* is by the choice of the patient; *involuntary* is by the choice of someone else (e.g., the doctor, patient's closest relative, proxy, or legally appointed representative) with concern for the patient's welfare

Journal Work: Exploring Assumptions

Write short answers to the following questions. Feel free to share your answers with a partner.

1. Do you think it is ever acceptable for someone to commit suicide? Why?
2. What moral assumptions are you making about human life in your answer?
3. Do you see an inherent moral distinction between active and passive euthanasia? If so, what is it?

Views on Human Life

Issues concerning suicide and active euthanasia highlight some of the more apparent differences between American secular, Christian (by and large Catholic in this case), and Jewish ideologies. American secular thought generally views humanity in utilitarian and pragmatic terms (i.e., usefulness), understanding human worth by what people can do for themselves or others. Hence the emphatic partiality toward people with "useful characteristics," such as youth, beauty, and wealth found in the media and pop culture icons. Also, the Declaration of Independence and American law claim that we each own our body and that we have the liberty to do with it as we will, as long as we do not harm another. Consequently, suicide is a legal act in all fifty states, although assisting someone in suicide is legal only in Oregon.[43]

In Christian ideology, there is a division between Protestants and Catholics on these issues. Protestants represent all possible points on the spectrum of attitudes, ranging from condemnation to advocacy. In contrast, the Catholic Church is explicit on such issues.

The teaching of the Church is unequivocal that God is the supreme master of life and death and that no human being is allowed to usurp His dominion so as deliberately to put an end to life, either his own or any one else's without authorization. . . . The Church has never allowed and never will allow the killing of individuals on grounds of private expediency; for instance . . . putting an end to prolonged suffering or hopeless sickness.[44]

Of course, this statement has to be understood in light of the Catholic theological underpinnings concerning the purposefulness of human suffering. That is, humans suffer as penance for their sins; humans endure pain for the spiritual good of their fellow humans, and suffering teaches humility.

Applying the Tradition

Suicide and euthanasia are by no means simple matters for Judaism, especially in light of recent medical and technological advances in sustaining life. There are significant differences among Reform, Conservative, and Orthodox Jews as to how to approach these matters and how to use the tradition in making such life and death decisions. There are certain relevant sources, however, that are most often included in discussions regarding the topics at hand.

Analyzing the Law

Analyze the following classical Jewish sources and answer the questions that follow them.

Jewish Source Material

- "They [Romans] took Rabbi Haninah ben Teradion, wrapped him in the scroll of the Torah, placed bundles and branches around him, and set them on fire. They then brought tufts of wool, which they had soaked in water, and placed them over his heart, so that he should not expire quickly. . . . His disciples said to him, 'Open your mouth so that the fire may penetrate.' He replied, 'Let Him who gave me [my soul] take it away, but no one should injure oneself.' The executioner then said to him, 'Rabbi, if I raise the flame and take away the tufts of wool over your heart, will you bring me to the life of the world to come?' 'Yes,' he replied. 'Then swear to me' [he urged]. He swore to him. He thereupon raised the flame and removed the tufts of wool from over his heart, and his soul departed speedily" (B. *Avodah Zarah* 18a).

- "One who is in a dying condition is regarded as a living person in all respects. . . . He who touches him [thereby accelerating his death] is guilty of shedding blood. . . . Whoever closes the eyes of a dying person while the soul is about to depart is shedding blood. One should wait a while; perhaps he is just in a swoon" (M.T. *Laws of Mourning* 4:5).

- "If a person is suffering from extreme pain and he says to another, 'You see that I shall not live [long]; kill me because I cannot bear the pain,' one is forbidden to touch him . . . whereas Saul [when he purposefully fell on his own sword] was permitted [to shorten his life] to prevent a desecration of the divine name before Israel. . . . If a person is suffering great pain and he knows that he will not live [long], he may not kill himself. And this we learn from Rabbi Haninah ben Teradion who refused to open his mouth [to allow the fire to enter and take his life]" (*Sefer Hasidim* 723–724).

- "It is forbidden to do anything to hasten the death of one who is in a dying condition. . . . If, however, there is something that causes a delay in the exit of the soul, as for example, if near to his house there is a sound of pounding as one who is chopping wood, or there is salt on his tongue, and these delay the soul's leaving the body, it is permitted to remove these because there is no direct act involved here, only the removal of an obstacle" (Rabbi Moses Isserles, "The Rema," on *Yoreh De'ah* 339:2).

Questions

If you are working individually, write your answers in your journal. If you are working with a group, share and discuss each other's responses.

1. According to these sources, is there a distinction between suicide, active euthanasia, and passive euthanasia? Which appears to be permitted and which is forbidden?

2. What are the inherent differences and similarities in terms of moral and theological assumptions between these sources and the Catholic statement presented earlier in this unit?

3. According to your answer in question 1, what might be some of the practical implications for current cases of terminally ill patients?

4. Do you agree with the implications of these sources? What do you believe Jewish law should be for suicide and euthanasia? Why?

Possible Answers

In the reading, Rabbi Dorff draws on many sources, including those presented above, and clearly articulates his understanding of Jewish law relating to suicide and euthanasia. With respect to suicide, he states that the "Jewish tradition prohibits suicide except as an act of martyrdom." Although euthanasia is a more complex issue, Rabbi Dorff holds that passive euthanasia is permitted: "Withdrawing or withholding life support from terminally ill patients is justified in Jewish law by its mandate that we not prolong the process of dying."[45]

Applying What You Read

A much harder question concerning euthanasia is posed when considering someone who is in persistent vegetative state (PVS). A PVS patient has no brain-wave activity and is sustained by heart and lung machines. Since the PVS patient has lost neocortical function, he or she is incapable of experiencing pain. The pertinent question is whether or not to remove the nutrition and hydration feeding tubes, as the patient cannot eat or drink on his or her own. In the reading for this unit, Rabbi Dorff presents two possible moral arguments for removal of these tubes. First, nutrition and hydration are equivalent to medicine in this case and, therefore, can be seen as an "obstacle" to death that may be removed. Second, following the medical community, which understands PVS patients to be brain dead (the neocortex has irreversibly lost its function), it is possible to simply classify such patients as dead; thus, removal of feeding tubes is permitted.

You Be the Judge

Individually or with a partner, read the following scenario and determine what you consider to be the most moral solution to the problem.

Scenario

Seven years ago in Stockton, California, Robert Wedland, now forty-eight years old, got "wildly drunk" and flipped his pickup truck, bringing his life to a "crashing halt." Today, he lies in Lodi Memorial Hospital, kept alive only by a tube that provides him with nutrition and hydration, because he is severely brain damaged. Wedland cannot walk, talk, eat, or communicate meaningful thoughts, if he still has any at all. Although he will never be the husband and father of his three children (ages sixteen, twenty, and twenty-two) that he once was, he is, however, occasionally able to perform a simple, zombie-like command, such as tossing a ball or placing a colored peg in a hole.

Robert's wife, Rose, wants to remove the tubes and allow Robert to die; even though he never wrote down his wishes for such a situation, Rose claims that this is what he wanted. On the other hand, despite the doctors' hopeless prognosis, Robert's mother, Florence, wants to keep him on the tubes, claiming that God "has a purpose for Robert—to help other people from having their tubes pulled." Florence believes that with enough therapy and prayer Robert can make progress. Rose counters, "The good Lord did take him. We're keeping him alive artificially." Rose and Florence have been battling each other on this for some time and will face each other in California's Supreme Court.

"Both sides agree on one thing, however: Had Robert kept a legal document outlining his specific wishes in the event of a catastrophic accident, it would have provided a much-needed voice for a sad, crippled man who now lies silent."[46]

After determining a moral solution to this problem, write your thoughts in the form of a letter to the California Supreme Court. Be sure to include the ideas and theories that support your solution. Feel free to share your letter with others.

Create a Medical Directive for Health Care

After reading the story of Robert Wedlend, we understand just how important it is to create a legal document outlining specific wishes in the event of a catastrophic accident. Some of us do not like to think of such possibilities, but we all know that they can happen. Some of us also have superstitions about writing down our wishes or even thinking about them, believing that we could bring a catastrophe on ourselves. Given these sensitivities and the wariness of the subject, this exercise may not be appropriate for everyone, particularly young teens. May we all reach 120.

Acquire copies, samples, or forms for Jewish medical directives for health care for yourself or for each person in your group. These sources offer guidance for end-of-life decision-making and ask about specific wishes if there is a catastrophe, such as who you will appoint as proxy for medical decisions and what to do in the case that you are terminally ill. Rabbi Dorff believes that it is extremely important to fill out the proper forms and that everyone should do this.

The following sources and publications, particular to each Jewish movement, are available:

- *Reform: A Time to Prepare,* edited by Rabbi Richard F. Address and the Commission on Jewish Family Concerns (published by Union of American Hebrew Congregations Press). [To order a copy: Voice: 888-489-8242 or 212-650-4121; fax: 212-650-4119; e-mail: press@uahc.org.]
- *Reconstructionist:* Behoref Hayamim—*In the Winter of Life: A Values-Based Guide for Decision Making at the End of Life,* compiled by the Reconstructionist Rabbinical College, Center for Jewish Ethics Staff (published by RRC Press). [To order a copy: On-line: available through several Web sites, including amazon.com.]
- *Conservative: Jewish Medical Directives for Health Care,* created by the Committee on Jewish Law and Standards of the Rabbinical Assembly. [To order a copy: Voice: 212-533-7800, ext. 2003; write: United Synagogue Book Service, 155 Fifth Avenue, New York, NY, 10010; on-line: www.uscj.org.]
- *Orthodox: Guide for the Jewish Hospital Patient,* by Rabbi David Weinberger, and *Illness and Crisis: Coping the Jewish Way,* by Rabbi Tsvi Schur. [To order a copy: On-line: www.ou.org/publications.]

Create an Ethical Will

Although this is an individual concern, it may be beneficial to complete an ethical will in a group so that group members have the opportunity to share what they have written. On pages 172–175 of the reading for this unit, Rabbi Dorff describes an ethical will. Take ten to fifteen minutes to write a rough draft of your ethical will. If you are working in a group and group members feel comfortable doing so, share the ethical wills so that members can learn from one another.

It may be helpful to read a sample ethical will to generate ideas about how to write your own. The book *Ethical Wills: A Modern Jewish Treasury,* by J. Riemer and N. Stampfler (New York: Schocken Books, 1983), is a good source.

Summary

Some people believe that because we die our lives are random occurrences without any significance. Others believe that because we die there is endless meaning in each moment and that there is tremendous significance in all that our eyes see and our hands do. Judaism teaches that life is a gift from God, evidence of our eternal soul that is precious and worth preserving.

However, Judaism also acknowledges that there are irreversible circumstances in which human suffering is unnecessary. These unfortunate cases test some of our fundamental assumptions about humanity; therefore, special moral considerations about the conditions of these situations must be made by either the one suffering or by his or her loved ones. Accordingly, it is more important than at any other time to work to make the best decisions possible for each invested party, precisely because these are the most difficult and heart-wrenching decisions that most of us will ever have to make. Too often, family and friends fight about the decisions they must make in the fleeting moments of a loved one's life. Judaism offers timeless moral assistance in coming to an ethical solution to these crises, passing on wisdom, preserving a relationship with God, and bringing peace of mind. Few life-cycle events outside death appeal more to our need of reasonable and faithful guidance.

Recommended Reading for Unit 11

Jakobovits, Immanuel. *Jewish Medical Ethics* (New York: Bloch, 1975).

Mackler, Aaron L., ed. *Life and Death Responsibilities in Jewish Biomedical Ethics* (New York: Jewish Theological Seminary, 2000). [See Chapters 15–26]

Washofsky, Mark. *Jewish Living: A Guide to Contemporary Reform Practice* (New York: UAHC Press, 2001). [See Chapter 6]

Unit 12 – Forgiveness: An Interpersonal Process

Reading

- *Love Your Neighbor and Yourself:* Chapter 6

Whetting Your Appetite

An integral part of being forgiving, and even being able to ask for forgiveness, is understanding both the obstacles to forgiving and the factors that prompt forgiveness. Some of us understand this intuitively, but others must consciously itemize the elements of forgiving and being forgiven. The exercise below helps illuminate some of the elements that act as obstacles to forgiving and some of the factors that prompt forgiveness.

Exercise

Read the story and answer the questions that follow it.

A former inmate of a Nazi concentration camp was visiting a friend who had shared the ordeal with him.

"Have you forgiven the Nazis?" he asked his friend.

"Yes."

"Well, I haven't. I'm still consumed with hatred for them."

"In that case," said his friend gently, "they still have you in prison."[47]

1. The friend compares failure to forgive to being in prison. Explain this comparison. In what ways is one who is not able to forgive in prison?
2. The story implies that the friend has forgiven the Nazis and is no longer in prison. What did he have to do to forgive them and free himself from that prison?
3. How do the obstacles to forgiving implied in this story compare to the ones Rabbi Dorff outlines in the reading for this unit? How do the factors that lead to forgiveness compare?

Making Mistakes

None of us is perfect. Parents, children, teachers, students, coworkers, employers, employees, clergymen, presidents of the United States, you, and I—not a single one of us is perfect. We have all made mistakes, and we will continue to make them. Despite how obvious and simple this concept appears to be, it may be the most difficult spiritual and psychological lesson that we have to learn in life. It is hard to admit that we have wronged other people, especially those who love us. It is just as hard, or even harder, to understand when someone else has wronged us. Our lack of understanding of our own imperfections makes it hard to ask for forgiveness, and the lack of understanding of others' imperfections makes it hard for us to forgive them.

It is interesting that Judaism teaches that we are imperfect, not because we are innately sinful—as in the Christian doctrine of Original Sin—but rather because we have free will and inclinations toward both good and evil (*yetzer ha-tov* and *yetzer ha-ra*). Judaism recognizes that we will occasionally stray off the right path and give in to the evil inclination, but we have the Torah as a guide, which can help prevent us from straying and which also helps us return to the proper path (*teshuvah*) when we do.

In the weekday *Amidah* (or *Ha-Tefilah,* meaning "The Prayer"), the central Jewish prayer, Jews acknowledge that we have the ability to distinguish right from wrong; that we sometimes choose the wrong; and that God, being compassionate and forgiving, wants our return. Reciting these acknowledgments, however, does not necessarily make it any easier either to ask for forgiveness or to be forgiving to another human being. It depends on how we understand those portions of the *Amidah* and on how seriously we take them.

Journal Work: Exploring Assumptions

Write short answers to the following questions. Feel free to share your answers with a partner.

1. Are you a forgiving person? How so?
2. Is it important to be forgiving? Why or why not?
3. Under what circumstances would you be prepared to forgive someone else?
4. What do you think you would need to do to be forgiven for wronging someone else?

A Jewish Approach

In Unit 2 we learned that, together with stories, models, maxims, and other things, Judaism uses law to determine moral behavior and to motivate us to be moral. In regard to forgiveness, the process is not merely an internal or psychological one; rather, it is a concrete interpersonal process by which the offender must actually do certain things to remedy the offense and compensate the victim, even if he or she does not want to.

Rabbi Dorff interprets this prescribed behavior from Maimonides' code of law, the *Mishneh Torah.* In the reading for this unit, he derives a list of eight basic elements involved in the process of forgiveness, including an honest acknowledgment of the wrongdoing, a public expression of remorse, compensation to the victim, and not repeating the offense when confronted with the same situation (p. 220).

You Be the Judge

Individually or with a partner, read the following scenarios and determine what moral course of action the offender should take to remedy the problem and be in accordance with Maimonides' elements of forgiveness.

Scenario 1

The Fisher women have a family quilt that is very meaningful. Six generations ago one of their ancestors knitted a white quilt. Ever since, each female member of the Fisher family has had the duty and honor to personalize a section of the quilt by sewing something onto it. This has become a rich family tradition that has been used to teach the family genealogy and to inspire family pride.

Lisa has just turned eighteen years old, and it is now her turn to personalize a section of the quilt. She has been working on it for two days, keeping the quilt in her room. This morning, after Lisa went to school, her younger brother, Phillip, went into her room to borrow a CD. Phillip entered the room, set down the can of cola that he was drinking, and quickly grabbed the CD. When he went to retrieve his drink, it slipped from his fingers and spilled onto Lisa's chair, where the quilt had been lying. The cola stained about half of the quilt. Although Phillip tried to clean it so that no one would discover what he had done, the stain was still very visible.

Determine the correct course of action for Phillip. Write it down. Feel free to share your thoughts with a partner.

Scenario 2

Julie and Zachary have been married for two years and have a nine-month-old baby. Zachary works at a local military base as a technological consultant. However, owing to the nature of his job, he is occasionally sent to other bases around the nation to train the personnel in new technology.

Last month, Zachary was sent away to a base in Virginia for three weeks. While he was there, he got involved in an affair with a woman who worked on that base. Zachary loves Julie very much and viewed the affair as "just playing around;" it was not serious and was not intended to be something lasting. When Zachary returned from Virginia, he realized just how much he truly loved Julie and their baby, and he vowed never do something like that again. However, the more time he spends with Julie and the baby, the more he feels guilty and troubled about what he did.

Determine the correct course of action for Zachary. Write it down. Feel free to share your thoughts with a partner.

Questions

1. Was it easy or difficult to apply a Jewish approach to morality in these scenarios? Why? What made it so?
2. Do you believe that this approach can work for every potential scenario, or are there circumstances for which such a model would not apply? If there are cases in which this approach does not apply, give an example and explain.

For Your Group

Values Identification

Divide into groups of two or three people. Instruct each group to read the following story and then create a Values Chart.

Values Chart

A Values Chart has concept categories that help demonstrate the complexity of the value expressed in the story. The basic setup of the chart is shown in Table 3.

Table 3. Values Chart

Concept Category	Comments
Value	
Similar values	
Benefits of the value	
Conflicting values	
Limitations of the value	

Next to the categories, each group writes what it considers to be the appropriate explanation, based on the following guidelines and remembering that there is no right or wrong way to fill out the Values Chart.

- *Value:* The primary value expressed by the story. This can include a dictionary definition or simply an indication of the area of human life to which the value refers (e.g., honesty: telling the truth, communication)
- *Similar values:* The values that support the primary value. This may include synonyms of the primary value or values that seem to be positively correlated to the primary value (e.g., honesty: courage, sincerity, friendship, trust)
- *Benefits of the value:* Benefits that might come from the primary value (e.g., honesty: knowledge of the truth, believing what people say)
- *Conflicting values:* Values that might conflict with the primary value (e.g., honesty: friendship, privacy, respect for others)
- *Limitations of the value:* Disadvantages, problems, or limits upholding the primary value (e.g., honesty: sometimes you should keep a secret, being impolite)

Here is the completed Values Chart based on the example primary value of "honesty."

Table 4. Values Chart: Example – "Honesty"

Concept Category	Comments
Value	honesty: telling the truth, communication
Similar values	courage, sincerity, friendship, trust
Benefits of the value	knowledge of the truth, believing what people say
Conflicting values	friendship, privacy, respect for others
Limitations of the value	sometimes you should keep a secret, being impolite

Story

Rabbi Elimelech of Lizensk was asked by a disciple how one should pray for forgiveness. He told him to observe the behavior of a certain innkeeper before Yom Kippur. The disciple took lodging at the inn and observed the proprietor for several days, but he could see nothing relevant to his quest. Then, one night before Yom Kippur, he saw the innkeeper open two large ledgers. From the first book he read off a list of all of the sins he had committed throughout the past year. When he finished, he opened the second book and proceeded to recite all the bad things that had occurred to him during the past year. When he had finished reading both books, he lifted his eyes to heaven and said, "Dear God, it is true I have sinned against You. But You have done many distressful things to me, too. However, we are now beginning a new year. Let us wipe the slate clean. I will forgive You, and You forgive me."[48]

After the groups have completed their Values Chart for the story, the charts should be shared with the whole group. Members can use the differences and similarities among the charts as a guide for discussion.

Journal Work: Reflection

Answer the following question. Feel free to share your answer with a partner.

1. How important in your life is forgiving others and being forgiven by others? Explain.

Summary

Asking for forgiveness and being forgiving are extremely difficult. Judaism teaches that God is compassionate and forgiving and that we should aspire to be like God by also being compassionate and forgiving. The conditions for forgiveness are confession, repentance, and the resolution to not repeat the same transgression. When the wrongdoer has completed the process of seeking forgiveness, the injured party should freely forgive injuries and offenses, for the transgressor has taken all means possible to rectify the wrong.

This formula, however, may not always work cleanly, depending on the situation and the type of transgression; for some, certain transgressions seem unforgivable (e.g., family violence, the Holocaust). Nonetheless, the Jewish approach to forgiveness implies that it is important to be aware of our moral values and to transform them into actions. While acts of forgiveness may never be easy and common, making Jewish values part of one's life can help minimize transgressions, especially extremely egregious ones, and repair the damage we do when we wrong someone else.

Recommended Reading for Unit 12

Kravitz, Leonard S., and Kerry M. Olitzky. *The Journey of the Soul: Traditional Sources on Teshuvah* (Northvale, NJ: Aronson, 1995).

Notes

1. If you are not familiar with abstract philosophy, you may want to begin with another unit and come back to this one later (see "Self Guidance" on p. 3).

2. Sarah Lyall, "Whites Have Black Twins in In-Vitro Mix-Up," July 9, 2002, A12.

3. Under the point system, this can be played like a group version of "Jeopardy." Each question is worth ten points, or the three questions can be scaled according to difficulty, so that there are ten-, fifteen-, and twenty-point questions. (The facilitator should arrange three stacks of questions accordingly.) One group can choose to answer the questions and the facilitator can act as the host of the game. He or she will control the point calculations as well as monitor correct and incorrect answers. The representative from the group that originally authored a specific question must be silent when one of their questions is asked to another group. If that representative assists the second group in answering his or her own question, ten points (or more) may be deducted from the responding group, depending upon the level of difficulty of the question being asked. If the responding group answers correctly, then that group receives the designated points. If they answer incorrectly, the question moves on to the next group in order.

4. *To Do the Right and the Good*, 13.

5. You may find it helpful to review the material in section E later in this unit before doing this exercise. Otherwise, once you have completed section E later in the unit, you may want to refer back to your responses to this exercise.

6. Biblical quotes are from the NJPS translation (1985), unless otherwise noted.

7. Note that Maimonides is suggesting that the origin of the tattooing prohibition was concerned with idolatry (i.e., tattooing pagan gods' names on the body).

8. *Matters of Life and Death*, 267–269.

9. For a good, in-depth explanation of the various movements within Judaism, I recommend Elliot N. Dorff, *Conservative Judaism: Our Ancestors to Our Descendants* (New York: United Synagogue Youth, 1996), 96–149.

10. Ernest Becker, *The Denial of Death* (New York: Free Press, 1973), 26.

11. These tenets are fully developed in *Matters of Life and Death,* chapter 2.

12. Tom Verducci, "Totally Juiced," *Sports Illustrated* June 3, 2002, 34-45.

13. *Matters of Life and Death,* 38.

14. B. Brown, "U.S. Births Rise for First Time in Eight Years; Births to Teenagers Still Falling," *Family Planning Perspectives* 32, no. 5 (September–October 2000). Available at www.guttmacher.org/pubs/journals/3226300.html; accessed January 16, 2003. "The number of births in the United States rose to 3,941,553 in 1998, marking a 2% increase from 1997 and the first increase since 1990."

15. Alan Guttmacher Institute, "Induced Abortion" [Fact Sheet], 2002. Available at www.agiusa.org/pubs/fb_induced_abortion.html; accessed January 16, 2003. "In 1997, 1.33 million abortions took place, down from an estimated 1.61 million in 1990. From 1973 through 1997, more than 35 million legal abortions occurred."

16. Presently, no "undue burdens" may be placed on a woman's right to obtain an abortion as long as the fetus is not viable; once the fetus is viable, states may restrict abortion as long as the health of the mother receives paramount protection.

17. Alan Guttmacher Institute, "Induced Abortion."

18. This scenario was presented in, "Abortion—Ending Fetal Life," in *When Life Is in the Balance: Life and Death Decisions in Light of the Jewish Tradition,* Barry D. Cytron and Earl Schwartz (New York: United Synagogue Youth, 1986), 77–78.

19. This scenario was presented in George W. Harris, "Fathers and Fetuses," *Ethics* 96 (1986). [Reprinted in *Morality and Moral Controversies: Readings in Moral, Social, and Political Philosophy,* ed. John Arthur] (Upper Saddle River, NJ: Prentice Hall, 2002), 229.

20. Rabbi Dorff discusses the causes of infertility in *Matters of Life and Death,* 45.

21. It is highly recommended that you read the appropriate sections in *Matters of Life and Death* to gain a full understanding of these treatments and their concerns.

22. F. Neuda, *Hours of Devotion,* trans. R. Vulture (Vienna: Schlesinger, c. 1900), 110. Adapted by Michele Klein. eds., *Studies on the Haggadah from the Teachings of Nechama Leibowitz* (New York: Urim, 2002), 43.

23. Yitshak Reiner and Shmuel Peerless eds., *Studies on the Haggadah from the Teachings of Nechama Leibowitz* (New York: Urim, 2002), 43. Ps. 119:99 is alternatively translated in NJPS as "I have gained more insight than all my teachers."

24. Sarna, Nahum M. 1991. *The JPS Torah Commentary: Exodus.* Philadelphia: Jewish Publication Society, 113.

25. *Love Your Neighbor and Yourself,* 156.

26. *Love Your Neighbor and Yourself,* chap. 7, n. 38, citing Donna Foote, "The War of the Wills," *Newsweek,* Fall–Winter Special Edition, 2000, 66–67.

27. Elliot Dorff, "Family Violence," in *Responsa 1991–2000: The Committee on Jewish Law and Standards of the Conservative Movement,* ed. Kassel Abelson and David J. Fine (New York: The Rabbinical Assembly, 2002), 783–784.

28. K. Daniel O'Leary, "Through a Psychological Lens: Personality Traits, Personality Disorders, and Levels of Violence," in *Current Controversies on Family Violence,* ed. Richard J. Gelles and Donileen R. Loseke (Newbury Park, CA: Sage, 1993), 7–27. O'Leary found that 60 percent of a sample of physically abusive men reported that they were victims of child abuse, and 70 percent of the physically abusive men reported that they were either victims of child abuse or witnesses to violence between their parents.

29. *To Do the Right and the Good,* 127.

30. Lev. 25:35 is alternatively translated in NJPS as "and you hold him."

31. Job 1:10 is alternatively translated in NJPS as "You have blessed his efforts."

32. *To Do the Right and the Good,* 150. Emphasis in the original.

33. *To Do the Right and the Good,* 138.

34. Ibid., 160.

35. From Elliot N. Dorff, *"You Shall Strengthen Them": A Rabbinic Letter on the Poor* (New York: Rabbinical Assembly, 1999), 47. Rabbi Dorff lists additional organizations on pages 47–50.

36. Antoine Henri de Jomini, *The Art of War* (London: Greenhill Press, 1996). Jomini (1779–1869) was a Swiss general who was a military writer and analyst of several wars, including the French revolutionary wars.

37. Note that in Deuteronomy there is no mention of women going out to war or being exempt, whereas the mishnah uses the language of Joel 2:16, which speaks of brides and grooms going out to prepare for an apocalyptic battle. Although the bride may have been obligated for war, some commentators understand this mishnah to say that the

bride simply goes out from the canopy while the groom goes off to war, and others say that she does go to war but to supply food and water to the soldiers.

38. Literally "to reduce the idolators."

39. *To Do the Right and the Good*, 168.

40. "A Prayer for Peace," *Siddur Sim Shalom,* (New York: Rabbinical Assembly, 1989), 417.

41. Retold on the basis of an Israeli captain's report that was reprinted in Dov Kenuhel, ed., *Gush Ezion Be-Milhamato* (Jerusalem: Department of Youth, Jewish Agency, 1957), 143.

42. Richard A. Wasserstrom, "On the Morality of War: A Preliminary Inquiry," *Stanford Law Review* 21, no. 6 (June 1969), 1627–1656. [Reprinted in John Arthur, ed., *Morality and Moral Controversies: Readings in Moral, Social, and Political Philosophy*, (Upper Saddle River, NJ: Prentice Hall, 2002), 111–121.]

43. *Matters of Life and Death*, 179. See also p. 370, n. 4.

44. I. M. Rabinowitch and H. E. McDermot, "Euthanasia," *McGill Medical Journal* 19 (1950), 150–151.

45. Review *Matters of Life and Death,* pages 180–207 for a complete analysis of Rabbi Dorff's decision and the moral reasoning that supports that decision.

46. Summarized from Jeffrey Ressner, "When a Coma Isn't One," *Time,* March 26, 2001, 62.

47. Retold by Anthony de Mello, *The Heart of the Enlightened: A Book of Story Meditations* (New York: Doubleday, 1989), 107.

48. After Abraham J. Twerski, *Living Each Day* (Brooklyn: Mesorah, 1988), 342.